Table Tennis

STEPS TO SUCCESS

Richard McAfee

HUMAN KINETICS

Library of Congress Cataloging-in-Publication Data

McAfee, Richard.
    Table tennis : steps to success / Richard McAfee.
        p. cm. -- (Steps to success sports series)
    ISBN-13: 978-0-7360-7731-6 (soft cover)
    ISBN-10: 0-7360-7731-6 (soft cover)
    I. Title.
    GV1005.M32 2009
    796.34'6--dc22

                            2009004824

ISBN-10: 0-7360-7731-6 (print)   ISBN-10: 0-7360-8527-0 (Adobe PDF)
ISBN-13: 978-0-7360-7731-6 (print)   ISBN-13: 978-0-7360-8527-4 (Adobe PDF)

The Web addresses cited in this text were current as of April 2009, unless otherwise noted.

Acquisitions Editor: Tom Heine; **Developmental Editor:** Cynthia McEntire; **Assistant Editor:** Scott Hawkins; **Copyeditor:** Patsy Fortney; **Proofreader:** Jim Burns; **Permission Manager:** Martha Gullo; **Graphic Designer:** Nancy Rasmus; **Graphic Artist:** Tara Welsch; **Cover Designer:** Keith Blomberg; **Photographer (cover):** Butterflyna.com; **Photographer (interior):** Neil Bernstein; **Visual Production Assistant:** Joyce Brumfield; **Photo Production Manager:** Jason Allen; **Art Manager:** Kelly Hendren; **Illustrator:** Alan L. Wilborn; **Printer:** Versa Press

We thank the Aurora Table Tennis Club in Aurora, Colorado, and the Pied Pipers House of Pong in Lakewood, Colorado, for assistance in providing the locations for the photo shoot for this book.

Human Kinetics books are available at special discounts for bulk purchase. Special editions or book excerpts can also be created to specification. For details, contact the Special Sales Manager at Human Kinetics.

Printed in the United States of America   10 9 8 7 6 5 4 3 2 1

The paper in this book is certified under a sustainable forestry program.

Human Kinetics
Web site: www.HumanKinetics.com

United States: Human Kinetics
P.O. Box 5076
Champaign, IL 61825-5076
800-747-4457
e-mail: humank@hkusa.com

Canada: Human Kinetics
475 Devonshire Road Unit 100
Windsor, ON N8Y 2L5
800-465-7301 (in Canada only)
e-mail: info@hkcanada.com

Europe: Human Kinetics
107 Bradford Road
Stanningley
Leeds LS28 6AT, United Kingdom
+44 (0) 113 255 5665
e-mail: hk@hkeurope.com

Australia: Human Kinetics
57A Price Avenue
Lower Mitcham, South Australia 5062
08 8372 0999
e-mail: info@hkaustralia.com

New Zealand: Human Kinetics
Division of Sports Distributors NZ Ltd.
P.O. Box 300 226 Albany
North Shore City
Auckland
0064 9 448 1207
e-mail: info@humankinetics.co.nz

To my wife, Diane, my daughter, Sarah, and my mom, Elizabeth—three wonderful women, whose love and support made it possible for me to have a career in sport.

◨ Contents

Climbing the Steps to Table Tennis Success   vii

The Sport of Table Tennis   ix

Key to Diagrams   xx

Step 1   **Preparing to Play**   1

Step 2   **Hitting Drive Strokes**   13

Step 3   **Understanding Spin and Footwork**   25

Step 4   **Executing Spin Strokes**   45

Step 5   **Serving**   71

Step 6   **Returning Serve**   97

Step 7   **Using the Five-Ball Training
                 System**   **115**

Step 8   **Understanding Styles of
                 Play and Tactics**   **139**

Step 9   **Playing Intermediate Strokes**   **149**

Step 10   **Performing Intermediate Serves**   **179**

Step 11   **Competing Successfully in
                 Tournaments**   **191**

Glossary   201

About the Author   203

◰ Climbing the Steps to Table Tennis Success

Table tennis is truly a lifetime sport. Visit any local table tennis club or tournament and you will find athletes aged 8 to 80 having the time of their lives competing together. Table tennis offers benefits to players of all ages. For young children, it is perhaps the best sport for quickly developing the eye–hand coordination so important for future physical development. For the competitive athlete, table tennis offers a range of tournament play from local competition all the way to the Olympic Games. The senior athlete will find the sport an excellent way to keep in shape, both physically and mentally. In the sport of table tennis, it is not so much your age, size, or physical ability or disability that matters most; it is the level of your skill. This book was written to give you the skills you will need to become a successful player.

This book offers a unique step-by-step approach to learning the sport of table tennis. Each step contains instruction, corrections to common mistakes, and scored drills. Your results in the drills will indicate whether you have mastered the new material and are ready to move on to the next step.

The steps here are presented in the same order I use when teaching my own classes and individual students. Each step builds on the material of the previous step. If you are new to table tennis, start at step 1 and work through the book. If you are an experienced tournament player, you may prefer to go directly to the area of instruction that most interests you.

Both beginning and intermediate players, as well as their teachers and coaches, will benefit from the information in *Table Tennis: Steps to Success*. Beginners will develop a strong founda-

tion in proper stroke technique, create their own style of play, and learn to use the most effective practice methods. Intermediate players will find a wide range of more advanced topics to help them take their games to the next level, along with a good review of the fundamentals. Anyone wishing to teach the sport will find a turnkey system of instruction.

The steps to success follow a proven developmental path for table tennis athletes. Early drills develop hand skills, and drills then progress to address all the basic forehand and backhand strokes. Through the use of clear instructions, innovative illustrations, and engaging photographs, this book teaches players the elements of spin, footwork, and effective practice for each new stroke technique. After mastering these basics, players can quickly begin to combine strokes to play points, using the unique five-ball training system. As players develop their strengths, they are then aided in developing their own personal styles of play based on their strongest strokes and physical skill sets.

For intermediate players, *Table Tennis: Steps to Success* offers a more thorough explanation of strokes than basic instructional books do. Descriptions of the three elements of each stroke—how to touch the ball, when to touch the ball, and where to touch the ball—will help players learn to correct mistakes as they move toward playing at a higher level. Intermediate players can also refine their styles, learn advanced strokes and tactics, and work toward successful tournament play.

For teachers and coaches, *Table Tennis: Steps to Success* provides a complete teaching package featuring step-by-step instruction, scored drills, and corrections for common mistakes. Also included are a brief history of the sport, up-to-date equipment information, an explanation of rules, warm-up and cool-down routines, Web-based table tennis resources, and a glossary.

Table Tennis: Steps to Success includes all recent rule and equipment changes, which have dramatically affected the sport. The move from the traditional 38-millimeter ball to the 40-millimeter ball has forced changes in stroke technique and styles of play. Perhaps the biggest change has been the move from 21-point games to 11-point games, a change that has forced major alterations in both serve and match tactics. To deal with these dramatic changes, *Table Tennis: Steps to Success* features the most up-to-date information on the serve–return game, as well as match tactics.

Table Tennis: Steps to Success provides a systematic approach to learning and playing table tennis. This system of instruction includes the following:

1. *Stroke instruction*. Steps 1 through 9 feature explanations of how to execute each stroke. Detailed illustrations and photos help you develop a strong mental picture of each stroke from the preparation to the contact point and follow-through. The three elements of all strokes—how to touch the ball, when to touch the ball, and where to touch the ball—are explained and clearly illustrated. As you learn how these elements work together, you will quickly be able to correct your own errors.

2. *Self-paced drills*. You should perform the drills in the order in which they appear. You may modify many drills to make them more or less difficult depending on your skill level.

3. *Success checks*. While executing each drill, read the success checks for a reminder of the key elements to focus on. Ask a coach, instructor, or seasoned player to observe you and evaluate your skill as you perform the drills.

4. *Score your success*. You earn points for each drill, depending on your performance. Repeat each drill as many times as you like, but don't obsess over getting a perfect score. Have fun and learn to enjoy the challenge the drills provide. The more you practice, the sooner you will see the results.

5. *Missteps*. No player has perfect technique, and players at all levels make common stroke errors. For each stroke, *Table Tennis: Steps to Success* offers examples of common errors and ways to correct them.

6. *Success summary*. A success summary at the end of each step highlights the key elements in that step. You also will be asked to rate your success based on your drill scores. By adding up the scores you attained on the drills, you will know whether you need more practice or are ready to move on to the next step.

Steps 7 through 11 help you move from recreational play into the world of tournament table tennis. Here you will find the advanced techniques, match tactics, and sport psychology tools necessary for becoming a successful match player. You will learn to adjust to playing against various styles by using drills and activities that simulate game and match situations.

Whether you are new to the game or an experienced player looking to sharpen your skills, the systematic approach offered in this book will work for you. Even advanced players will find drills that challenge their skills and tactical tips that will give them the edge over their opponents. For teachers and coaches, *Table Tennis: Steps to Success* is the most up-to-date, comprehensive resource available.

Your reward for completing all the steps is the fulfillment of your own personal goals. Whether you just want to have more fun playing with your friends or want to compete on a local, regional, or even national level, *Table Tennis: Steps to Success* can help you achieve your goals.

◨ The Sport of Table Tennis

In a little over 120 years, the sport of table tennis has steadily risen from an after-dinner pastime to one of the world's major participation sports. This remarkable growth is due in large part to the fact that it is a safe, fun, healthy, and truly lifetime activity.

HISTORY OF TABLE TENNIS

The history of table tennis parallels the evolution of its equipment, which is common in many sports. The first references to the game appeared in the 1890s with early attempts to develop an indoor version of tennis. The game went by many names and was played on dining tables as a popular after-dinner entertainment. The game was played with long-handled rackets covered with velum and balls of cork or rubber. The poor quality of the balls largely led to the quick demise of these early forms of the game.

With the development of the celluloid ball in the 1920s, the game slowly began to revive. Several major game companies, such as J. Jacques & Son in England and Parker Brothers in the United States, began to successfully promote competing versions of the game under a variety of names. In the United States, the Parker Brothers trademark of Ping Pong was the most widely accepted. The game also began to grow in sport clubs throughout Europe. In 1927, the International Table Tennis Federation (ITTF) was formed, and the first world championships were conducted.

With the invention of the hard rubber racket in the 1930s, the game took a major leap forward. This racket has a layer of rubber with short, hard pimples that cover the wood blade. For the first time, players could apply a moderate amount of spin to the ball, and spin strokes were developed. This allowed far more ball control and speed. The game quickly grew in popularity with the establishment of league play throughout Europe and clubs in the United States. The United States Table Tennis Association (USTTA) was formed in 1933. Although European players dominated during this era, the U.S. team was very competitive and won several world titles.

The modern game began with the introduction of the sponge bat in the 1950s. After much experimentation, the current restrictions of rubber over a sponge layer (pimples in or out) with a maximum thickness of 4 millimeters was decided on. The Japanese, with their penhold grip, long and powerful strokes, and great footwork, were the first to capitalize on the greatly increased spin and speed that this equipment afforded. They would dominate the sport through much of the 1950s and early 1960s. The Chinese emerged on the scene in the early 1960s and quickly took over as the sport's great innovators and begin a period of dominance that continues today. They pioneered the fast-attack style of play and showed the world the importance of developing a strong serve and serve–return game. Although China has dominated the sport in recent years, many players from other Asian nations and many European players have broken through to gain individual world and Olympic titles.

Table tennis made its Olympic debut at the Seoul Olympics in 1988, at which point it gained true worldwide recognition. National Olympic committees from around the world began pouring money and support into creating medal contenders, and the overall caliber of play rose everywhere. Since that time, continual advancements in equipment have led to faster and faster play. As in all sports, the professional table tennis athlete has had to become bigger, stronger, and faster.

Table tennis is now one of the largest participation sports in the world. The ITTF consists of 204 member countries. The ITTF conducts many world events including yearly world championships, world cups, and an international pro tour. Along with these events, the ITTF conducts an international junior development program consisting of camps, an international junior circuit, and world junior and cadet championships. There are also more than 100 yearly development courses conducted worldwide, offering training for coaches, officials, and athletes.

USA Table Tennis (formerly the USTTA) is the governing body for table tennis in the United States. It consists of a network of hundreds of local clubs and sanctioned tournaments. More than 17 million people in the United States play table tennis on a recreational level, but only about 50,000 play in organized club settings. Of these, more than 7,000 take part in competitions. When you compare this number to the more than 20 million serious players in China, or the almost one million participants in the German national league, it is clear that the United States has a long way to go to become competitive with the rest of the world.

With strong professional leagues existing throughout much of Europe and Asia, along with the ITTF pro tour, more and more professional athletes are making a good living playing table tennis. Although China continues to hold its lead, winning many of the world's major titles, the rest of the world is narrowing the gap.

EQUIPMENT

When selecting equipment, it is a good idea to look for items that have been approved by the ITTF and carry its logo. The use of approved equipment is mandatory for sanctioned tournament play. Also, this will ensure that you receive good-quality materials. To play table tennis, you need a racket (a blade covered with rubber), a table, a net set, balls, glue for rubbers, shoes, and proper clothing.

Blades

Table tennis blades must be composed mostly of wood (85 percent) and can include composite materials such as graphite. Head sizes vary somewhat (figure 1); defensive players often use blades with slightly larger head sizes. Close-to-the-table attackers often prefer more compact blades for quicker movement. Mid-distance players prefer the normal-sized blades.

Figure 1 Table tennis blades of various head sizes.

Most manufacturers market blades according to speed (figure 2). The speed rating refers to how much speed that particular blade will add to the ball at contact. In general, the faster the blade is, the lower the amount of control that blade will offer.

Blades come with a variety of handle shapes. When selecting a blade, make sure the handle shape is comfortable in your hand. The most popular handle shapes are the flared, straight, and anatomical (double flared). Although selecting a handle is mostly a matter of personal preference, if you tend to change your grip a good deal between your forehand and backhand strokes, you may find the straight handle easier to make the change with. Most blades weigh 80 to 90 grams without rubber.

Rubbers

The large variety of rubber coverings has made possible a wider variety of styles of play than exist in other racket sports. Because of the large variety of coverings available, a player normally buys the blade and rubbers separately. The rubbers are then attached using approved glues that allow for easy removal and replacement. Most often the store or dealer you buy from will assemble the racket for you, but it is a good skill for all players to learn. Most rubber coverings have a sponge layer under them to provide more spin and speed. The total thickness of the rubber and the sponge cannot exceed 4 millimeters. By rule, all rackets used in any official tournament play must have black rubber on one side and red on the other.

The four general types of rubber surfaces (figure 3) are short pips, long pips, antispin, and inverted. The word *pip* refers to a raised bump, typically with a conic shape, on the rubber sheet. *Short-pips* rubber has short, wide pips that face outward and are spaced closely together. Short pips can produce a moderate amount of spin on the ball. This rubber is used most often for blocking and hitting strokes. This type of rubber is also used by players who have weaker backhands and are looking for more control against their opponents' spin.

Figure 2 Blade with speed rating.

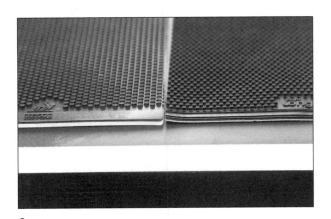

a

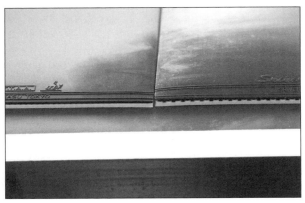

b

Figure 3 The four types of rubber coverings: *(a)* short pips and long pips; *(b)* antispin and inverted.

Long-pips rubber has longer and thinner pips that face out and bend easily on contact with the ball. Long pips have the unique effect of returning some of the opponent's spin to him, creating a tricky element. This, along with slower speed, makes long-pips rubber primarily a defensive rubber. It is not recommended for beginners.

Antispin rubber has a slick, smooth surface that removes most of the spin from the ball. Its lack of ability to produce spin makes attacking very difficult. It is used most often by defensive players on one side of the racket only to provide steady returns of an opponent's attacks.

Inverted rubber is the most popular type of rubber. It features a smooth top surface with the pips facing downward attached to a layer of sponge rubber. Inverted rubber offers the greatest range of spin and speed possibilities and is used by the majority of players. Manufacturers market inverted rubber with spin and speed ratings. As with blades, the faster the rubber is, the more difficult it is to control.

It is important to note that a blade can have two types of rubbers to support different types of play between backhand and forehand strokes.

Table tennis glues, which are used to attach rubbers to blades, are available from all major manufacturers. These special glues allow for the easy removal and replacement of rubbers. In 2008, the ITTF banned the use of all glues that contained volatile organic compounds (VOCs). These glues are being replaced by water-based glues.

Balls

Table tennis made a major change in 2000 by increasing the size of the ball from 38 millimeters to 40 millimeters. The reason for this change was to improve ball visibility on television.

Tournament-quality balls are available in white or orange and are marked *ITTF Approved 3-Star*. For practice and club play, one- and two-star balls are available at lower prices. Approved balls are tested for roundness, hardness, and a consistent bounce. High-quality balls last longer than lower-quality balls but still should be replaced when the surface becomes slick.

Tables and Nets

All regulation tables are 9 × 5 feet (274 × 152 cm) and stand 2 1/2 feet (76 cm) high (figure 4). When buying a table, look for a minimum of 3/4 inch (1.9 cm) in thickness. Table tops are made from highly compressed particle board and finished with a number of coats of special paint to produce a consistent bounce. Tables that are USATT or ITTF approved are high in quality and have been tested and proved to meet tournament standards in regard to height and consistency of bounce. All tables have a white line defining the side and end lines as well as a white center line.

Good-quality nets are usually made of cloth and have a cord through the top part to allow the tension to be adjusted. They are attached to the table by the use of metal net posts. When attached, the net is 6 inches (15 cm) high and the net posts extend 6 inches (15 cm) to the side of the table. ITTF-approved tables and nets are of higher quality than those that are not approved.

Ball-Throwing Machines, or Robots

One of the most helpful practice tools you can have is a ball-throwing machine, also commonly called a robot. Even the least expensive models throw one type of spin to a set location or random locations at various speeds and frequencies. More expensive models are computerized and can change the spin, location, and speed on each ball to simulate an actual point. Given that practice partners are not always available, I highly recommend the use of robots. Because most come with a net and automatically recycle balls, you can get maximum practice in a short time period.

Court

The table is the target that you and your opponent must land your shots on, whereas the court is the area you have to move around in. Minimum court size for tournament play is 7 × 14 meters (approximately 23 × 45 ft) with a minimum ceiling height of 5 meters (16.4 ft).

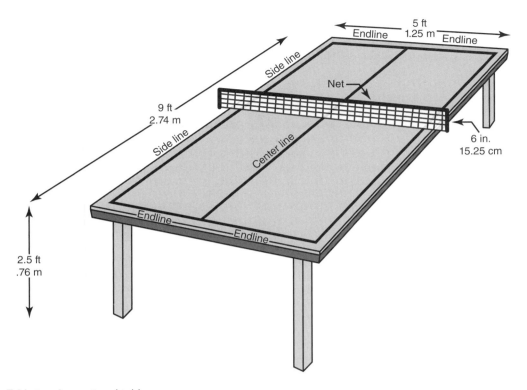

Figure 4 Table tennis court and table.

In regard to court size, more is better. In world championships and Olympic competition, the courts are often 8 × 16 meters (26 × 52 ft) with a ceiling height of 9 meters (30 ft) or more.

The minimum court lighting requirement for tournaments is 600 lux of uniform lighting over the playing area. For world championships and Olympic competitions, the minimum is 1,000 lux. The relatively small size of a table tennis ball makes lighting a key factor for the enjoyment of the game. Even for recreational play, the more light you have, the better.

Apparel

Any good-quality indoor court shoe will work well for table tennis. Table tennis shoes are available and, in general, are lighter in weight than most court shoes. Table tennis shoes are similar in design to volleyball shoes and normally are very lightweight and flexible and have a gum rubber sole.

Table tennis clothing (figure 5) is available from many manufacturers and consists of shorts

Figure 5 Players dressed for competition.

or skirt, shirt, and warm-up suit. However, any type of tennis clothing will work. Clothing that is the same color as the ball being used is not legal in tournament play. In tournament play, doubles teams normally play in matching outfits. In international events, opponents and doubles teams must wear different colors.

OFFICIAL RULES

All games are played to 11 points, but the winner must win by 2 points. The winner is the first person to reach 11 points or to go up by 2 points if both players are at or over 10 points. A match is any odd number of games. Matches usually are best of five or best of seven games.

In competition play, the choice of who serves first is decided by a coin toss. Often in club play one player holds a ball in one hand and hides both hands under the table. The opponent tries to guess which hand the ball is in. The winner then chooses either to serve first or receive first or to start at a particular end. Whoever receives first in one game serves first in the next game.

The serve alternates with each player serving twice until the game is over or until the score reaches 10–10. When the score is 10–10, serve alternates with each player serving once until one player has a 2-point lead.

You are awarded a point when any of the following occurs:

- Your opponent, who is serving, fails to make a good service.
- Your opponent, who is receiving the serve, fails to make a good return.
- Your opponent's return fails to touch your side of the table before it passes beyond the end line.
- The ball bounces twice on the table before your opponent returns it.
- Your opponent strikes the ball twice before returning it.
- Your opponent moves the table.
- Your opponent's free hand touches the playing surface.

A good serve starts with the ball resting freely in the open palm of the server's free hand. From the beginning of the serve, the ball must be above the level of the table and behind the end line and must not be hidden from the receiver by any part of the server's body (figure 6). The server throws the ball up near vertical at least 6 inches (15 cm) from the hand and strikes while it is descending. The serve first must touch the server's side of the table and then pass over or around the net and touch the receiver's side of the table. During the serve, if the ball touches the net or the net assembly but is otherwise a good serve, a *let* is called and the serve is replayed.

In doubles the partners alternate returning the ball during play. At the beginning of the first game, the team that has the right to serve decides who will serve first. The receiving pair chooses who will receive serve. After each 2

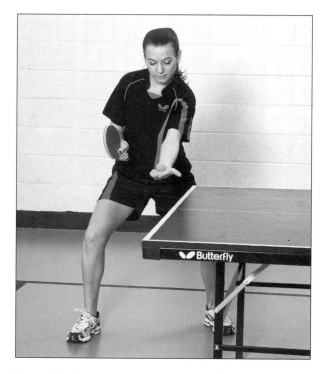

Figure 6 The server is ready to serve. The ball is above the level of the table, behind the endline, and not obstructed by the server's body.

points, the receiving player becomes the new server and the partner of the previous server becomes the new receiver. In doubles all serves first must bounce inside the server's right-hand box, which is formed by the middle line and the right side line on the table, and then travel crosscourt and bounce inside the receiver's right-hand box.

You can acquire a complete set of rules at the USA Table Tennis (USATT) Web site or the International Table Tennis Federation (ITTF) Web site. See the Resources section on page xix.

UNWRITTEN RULES

Like all sports, table tennis has unwritten rules you should know. This code of conduct includes both common etiquette and good sportsmanship concepts that are the accepted practices of the sport.

- The server should announce the score before each point, giving the server's score first.

- In matches without an umpire, each player is responsible for calling his side of the table, determining whether a ball hit or missed the table.

- Spectators should not be involved in the match and should not be solicited for their opinion about whether a ball was good or not.

- If a dispute arises, try to settle the argument with your opponent. If this is not possible, ask for an umpire.

- If a ball rolls into your court, immediately call a let. If you continue to play the point, you cannot call a let after the point is over.

- If your ball rolls onto an adjoining court, wait until play is over at that table before asking for your ball back.

- Shake hands with your opponent after the match.

- Avoid walking behind players when a point is in progress.

- Spectators should feel free to applaud or cheer winning shots but should refrain from cheering when a player makes an error.

WARMING UP, COOLING DOWN, AND STRETCHING

When engaging in any exercise or sport, you must warm up properly to prepare your body for exercise and avoid injuries. It is just as important to cool down after practice to help your body recover more quickly. Both warm-up and cool-down sessions should be combined with stretching exercises to increase muscle suppleness.

The purpose of a warm-up routine is to increase body heat gradually to prepare it for heavier exercise. A table tennis warm-up can consist of a few minutes of light jogging mixed with table tennis–specific movements such as side-to-side jumps and bounding movements. After warming up for 5 to 10 minutes, switch the focus to stretching.

Table tennis players must have loose and very flexible muscles to achieve the quick, explosive movements required by the sport. Stretching is an important part of any table tennis training session. Stretching also helps reduce the risk of muscle injuries. To stretch safely, do the following:

- Try to hold each stretch for 20 seconds.

- Do not bounce while stretching.

- Stretch slowly to the point of tension; you should never feel pain.

- Focus on your breathing while stretching.

- Select stretches that work all major muscle groups.

Your stretching session should last about 15 minutes.

• *Quadriceps stretch*. From a standing position with feet together, bend your left knee and raise your left foot toward your back as high as comfortable. Grasp your left foot with your left hand and gently lift until you feel the stretch in your left quadriceps (figure 7). Hold for 20 seconds. Relax and return your left foot to the floor. Repeat, stretching the right quadriceps.

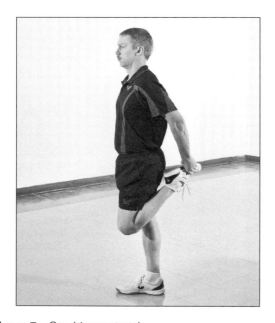

Figure 7　Quadriceps stretch.

• *Standing calf stretch*. Stand facing a wall or table tennis table about an arm's distance away. Reach out and put both hands on the wall or table while bending your right leg. Slowly slide your left leg back, keeping your foot flat on the floor, until you feel a comfortable stretch in your left calf muscle (figure 8). Hold the stretch for 20 seconds. Relax, bringing your left leg back even with your right. Repeat, stretching your right calf.

Figure 8　Standing calf stretch.

• *Standing hamstring stretch*. Stand facing a table tennis table. Raise your left leg and set it on the table. Reach both hands toward your left foot, slowly reaching toward your foot until you feel a comfortable stretch in your left hamstring (figure 9). Hold for 20 seconds. Relax and return to a standing position. Repeat, stretching your right hamstring.

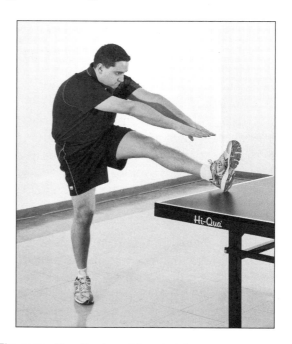

Figure 9　Standing hamstring stretch.

• *Hip flexor stretch.* From a standing position, lunge forward on your right leg (figure 10). Keep your back straight and tuck your bottom under. Hold the stretch for 20 seconds. Relax and return to the standing position. Repeat, lunging forward on your left leg.

Figure 10   Hip flexor stretch.

• *Lumbar extension and abdominal stretch.* Lie on the floor with your palms on the ground. Slowly push yourself up, bending at the waist until you feel a comfortable stretch in the lumbar region (figure 11). Hold for 20 seconds. Relax and return to the starting position.

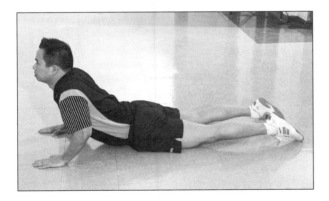

Figure 11   Lumbar extension and abdominal stretch.

• *Adductor stretch.* From a standing position with feet pointing forward, lunge sideways to your right until you feel a comfortable stretch (figure 12). Hold for 20 seconds. Repeat, lunging to the left.

Figure 12   Adductor stretch.

• *Supraspinatus stretch.* From a standing position, drop your right arm behind your neck. Grasp your right elbow with your left hand and pull your right arm to the left until you feel a comfortable stretch (figure 13). Hold for 20 seconds. Repeat, pulling your left arm to the right.

Figure 13   Supraspinatus stretch.

• *Biceps stretch.* From a standing position, extend both arms back behind your body. Slowly lift both arms until you feel a comfortable stretch in your biceps (figure 14). Hold for 20 seconds.

Figure 15 Triceps stretch.

Figure 14 Biceps stretch.

• *Triceps stretch.* From a standing position, raise your right elbow so that your right arm drops behind your neck. If you can reach, grasp your right hand with your left hand and gently pull until you feel a comfortable stretch in your right triceps. If you have trouble reaching your hand, use a towel stretched between your hands for the stretch (figure 15). Hold for 20 seconds. Repeat, stretching your left triceps.

• *Neck extension and flexion.* From a standing position, tilt your head forward until you feel a comfortable stretch. Hold for 20 seconds. Tilt your head back until you feel a comfortable stretch. Hold for 20 seconds. Tilt your head to the left until you feel a comfortable stretch. Hold for 20 seconds. Finally, tilt your head to the right until you feel a comfortable stretch (figure 16). Hold for 20 seconds. Do not force these stretches or use your hands to add force.

Immediately after the training or playing session, take the time to cool down properly. Start

Figure 16 Neck extension and flexion, head tilted to right.

with several minutes of light jogging or walking and move into 5 to 10 minutes of stretching. The purpose of the cool-down is to help the muscles recover more quickly and allow you to return to competition or training sooner.

INJURIES

Table tennis is a very safe sport. However, overuse injuries such as blisters, sprains, strains, cramps, and even tennis elbow are not uncommon. Most of these problems can be treated by the use of the RICER regime.

RICER stands for

Rest the injured part.

Ice; apply for 20 minutes every 2 to 3 hours for the first 48 hours.

Compression; apply a firm bandage over the injured part.

Elevation; raise the injured part above the level of the heart, if possible.

Referral; have a trained professional evaluate the injury.

The most important element in injury prevention is to develop proper warm-up and cooldown routines.

RESOURCES

You can get complete information about international table tennis from the International Table Tennis Federation (ITTF) Web site: www.ITTF.com.

USA Table Tennis (USATT) is the nonprofit national governing body for table tennis in the United States. Members of the USATT support the association's efforts to grow table tennis in the United States. The USATT consists of approximately 300 clubs throughout the United States. USATT members can take part in hundreds of tournaments each year and receive an excellent bimonthly magazine filled with articles, tournament results, player ratings, and coaching articles. Learn more about the USATT at www.USATT.org.

The Asian Table Tennis Union (ATTU) is recognized as the governing body for all Asian countries by the ITTF. The ATTU conducts many competitions and programs throughout Asia. Information is available at www.attu.org.

The European Table Tennis Union (ETTU) is recognized as the governing body for some 57 countries in Europe with more than four million active players taking part in its programs and competitions. For more information see the ETTU's Web site at www.ettu.org.

The following are some of the larger suppliers of table tennis equipment in the United States:

www.butterflyonline.com

www.newgy.com

www.paddlepalace.com

www.killerspin.com

www.joolausa.com

http://ttpioneers.ping-pong.com

www.espintech.com/home

www.zeropong.com

www.colestt.com

Key to Diagrams

→	Path of ball
▯	Racket
○	Ball
FH	Forehand
·····>	Ball rotation
⇒	Air resistance
(R)	Right foot
(L)	Left foot
– – →	Player movement
L R	Initial position
BH	Backhand
⊗	Ball bounce
▪	Target

Preparing to Play

Before beginning on-the-table training, you must learn some of the basic elements of the game and master a few hand skills. Taking time to understand these basic concepts will pay big dividends by allowing you to develop your skill at a faster pace.

GRIPPING THE RACKET

The first decision every player has to make is what grip to use on the racket. Your choice of a grip will play a major role in every part of your game, so let's take a look at your choices. There are two main grip styles: the shake-hands grip and the pen-hold grip. Their names describe them very accurately.

Shake-Hands Grip

The shake-hands grip is formed by grasping the blade between your thumb and forefinger and wrapping the remaining fingers around the handle (figure 1.1). The racket becomes a natural extension of your hand.

Figure 1.1 Shake-hands grip.

Misstep
Two fingers are on the blade.
Correction
Move the second finger to the handle, leaving only the forefinger on the blade.

When holding the racket, always use a relaxed grip. The only pressure points are the forefinger and thumb; the rest of the fingers loosely rest on the handle. When you use forehand strokes, the pressure from your forefinger controls the racket. When executing backhands, pressure from the thumb helps control the racket.

Misstep

There is too much tension in the hand.

Correction

Hold the blade lightly with only a small amount of pressure between the thumb and forefinger.

Players who use the shake-hands grip vary how high up on the racket they grip. In general, the higher up toward the blade you grip, the more control you have (figure 1.2a). The lower you grip, the more spin variation you can create (figure 1.2b). No matter where you feel comfortable gripping the blade, you always want to feel as though you are holding the blade and not the handle.

The shake-hands grip allows for the development of equally powerful backhand and forehand strokes. This grip has always been the predominant choice in Western countries, but is now the most popular grip in Asia as well. Several variations of the shake-hands grip have proven to be successful.

Neutral Grip

The neutral grip (figure 1.3) is a basic shake-hands grip, with the racket becoming a direct extension of the hand. This grip gets its name because it produces a neutral angle (the racket is straight up and down) for both backhand and forehand strokes. The neutral grip supports every kind of stroke and requires no grip change between forehand and backhand strokes. I strongly recommend this grip for new players.

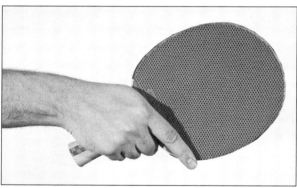

a

b

Figure 1.2 *(a)* High shake-hands grip; *(b)* low shake-hands grip.

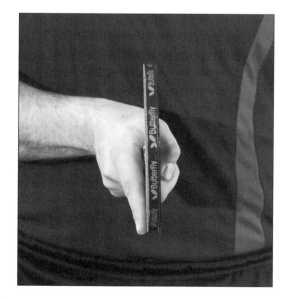

Figure 1.3 Neutral grip.

Strong Forehand Grip

The strong forehand grip produces a somewhat closed racket face on all forehand strokes. If you are a right-handed player, rotate the V between the thumb and forefinger from the top of the handle slightly to your right (figure 1.4). This grip supports strong forehand strokes, but puts the racket in a weak position for the backhand.

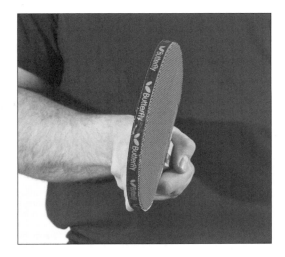

Figure 1.4   Strong forehand grip.

 Misstep
The forefinger is up the middle of the blade.
Correction
Move the forefinger down to the edge of the blade.

Misstep
The hand is holding only the handle of the blade (hammer grip).
Correction
Move the thumb and forefinger up onto the blade.

Strong Backhand Grip

The strong backhand grip is the opposite of the strong forehand grip. It produces a closed racket face on all backhand strokes (figure 1.5). In this case, a right-handed player rotates the V between the thumb and forefinger from the top of the handle slightly to the left. This grip supports strong backhand strokes, but puts the racket in a weaker position for the forehand.

Figure 1.5   Strong backhand grip.

 Misstep
The thumb is up the middle of the blade.
Correction
Only the side of the thumb, not the tip of the thumb, should touch the blade.

Pen-Hold Grip

The pen-hold grip is formed by holding the racket like a pen, with the thumb and forefinger on the same side of the racket and the rest of the fingers on the other side (figure 1.6). Again, the controlling pressure points are the thumb and forefinger.

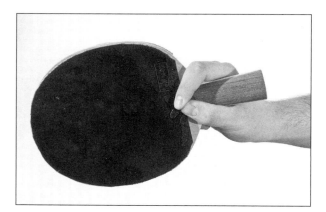

Figure 1.6 Pen-hold forehand grip.

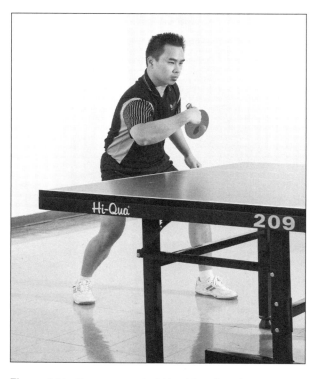

Figure 1.7 Reverse pen-hold backhand stroke.

Traditionally, players who used this grip used only one side of the racket for both forehand and backhand strokes. When hitting a forehand stroke, the player exerts slight downward pressure with the thumb. When hitting a backhand stroke, the player exerts downward pressure with the forefinger and makes a forward push with the fingers on the back of the racket.

The pen-hold grip allows for a greater range of wrist motion, which supports strong serves and forehand strokes. The weakness of this grip has always been the lack of reach on the backhand side. This has forced pen-hold players to play a predominantly forehand attacking game. To overcome this backhand weakness, many players use the reverse pen-hold backhand (figure 1.7). This new style, which uses both sides of the racket, has allowed pen-hold players to develop powerful backhand topspin strokes and has revitalized this grip at the world-class level.

This style of grip has long been very popular in Asia, and many world and Olympic champions have been pen-hold players. There are two major variations of the pen-hold grip: the Japanese, or Korean, style and the Chinese style.

Japanese, or Korean, Pen-Hold Grip

The Japanese, or Korean, pen-hold grip is defined by the spreading of the fingers on the reverse side of the blade (figure 1.8). This grip supports strong forehand play, but makes it difficult to use the wrist on the backhand. Players using this grip normally cover most of the table with their powerful forehands and simply block on their backhand sides.

Figure 1.8 Japanese, or Korean, pen-hold backhand grip.

Chinese Pen-Hold Grip

The Chinese pen-hold grip uses the three fingers on the reverse side. The fingers are curled (figure 1.9). This allows for much more use of the

Figure 1.9 Chinese pen-hold backhand grip.

wrist on both backhand and forehand strokes. Chinese pen-hold players often vary their finger position to better support a variety of strokes. This is especially true for those who are using the reverse backhand stroke.

Grip Choice

You can become a successful player with any of the preceding grips. Every grip has both strengths and weaknesses. Every technique you will learn in this book will work with any of these proven grips. If you are a new player and unsure about which grip to use, I suggest you start with the neutral shake-hands grip because it is the easiest to master.

Whatever your choice of grip, spend time practicing the grip and learning to control the ball with it. Ball-bouncing drills are a fun and effective way to accomplish both.

Ball Control Drill. *Ball Bouncing*

Practice each of the 10 ball control exercises. For each exercise, bounce the ball 20 times on the racket. Record the number of bounces you were able to complete successfully. Be sure to use the correct grip while completing these exercises.

1. Bounce the ball using the forehand side of the racket.

2. Bounce the ball using the backhand side of the racket.

3. Alternate, bouncing the ball once on the backhand side of the racket and once on the forehand side.

4. Bounce the ball once on the forehand side of the racket and once on the edge of the racket.

5. Volley the ball against a wall using the forehand side of the racket.

6. Volley the ball against a wall using the backhand side of the racket.

7. Volley the ball against a wall alternating between the forehand side of the racket and the backhand side.

8. Bounce the ball on the floor using the forehand side of the racket.

9. Bounce the ball on the floor using the backhand side of the racket.

10. Bounce the ball on the floor alternating between the forehand side of the racket and the backhand side.

Success Check

- Make sure you are using a proper shake-hands or pen-hold grip when executing the drill.
- Focus on controlling your blade by applying pressure with your forefinger and thumb.

Score Your Success

Bounce the ball 20 times during each of the 10 ball control exercises. Record the number of bounces you are able to complete in all 10 exercises.

180 to 200 bounces = 10 points

160 to 179 bounces = 8 points

140 to 159 bounces = 6 points

120 to 139 bounces = 4 points

100 to 119 bounces = 2 points

Your score ___

GETTING IN A READY POSITION

Another critical element to master is a good basic stance that will allow you to easily move into position to execute any stroke. Stand with your feet at least shoulder-width apart. A tall player will need an even wider stance. If you are right-handed, place your right foot slightly behind your left foot. If you are left-handed, your left foot should be slightly behind the right. Bend your knees and shift your weight to the front part of your feet. You will feel a slight forward lean when in the proper position. Finally, hold your racket straight ahead at the midpoint between the forehand and backhand (figure 1.10). In relation to the table, stand so you are covering about two-thirds of the table with your forehand. Stand at about arm's length behind the end line.

Figure 1.10 Ready Position

1. Feet shoulder-width apart or wider
2. Feet staggered, right foot slightly behind left
3. Knees bent
4. Weight on front of feet
5. Racket straight, midway between forehand and backhand
6. Arm's length behind end line

A good ready position accomplishes several things. First, it lowers your center of gravity, which allows you to move quickly while keeping good balance. The bent knees and forward lean allow you to transfer your weight easily into your strokes to create power. Also, instead of having you look down at the incoming ball, the low position helps you better see the ball as it comes toward you.

Players of different styles of play adjust this basic position to meet their needs. However, the basic ready position is perfect for learning all the basic strokes of the game.

MASTERING THE THREE BASIC ELEMENTS OF ALL STROKES

All table tennis strokes have three guiding principles in common. To execute any stroke, you have to know how to touch the ball, when to touch the ball, and where to touch the ball.

How to Touch the Ball

Every time you touch the ball with the racket, you impart energy to the ball. This energy takes the form of speed or spin. The application of speed or spin to a ball is controlled by how you touch the ball. The two general ways to touch the ball with the racket are force contact and friction contact.

Force contact occurs when the forward-moving racket strikes the ball. To experience this type of contact, try this simple drill. Using the correct grip, hold your racket out in front of you with your palm up (figure 1.11*a*). Bounce the ball on the racket as the racket moves a few inches (or centimeters) up and down (figure 1.11*b* and *c*). Watch the ball carefully as you hit straight through the ball. The ball will not spin because all of your energy is going into the forward movement of the ball. You also will notice a distinct sound coming from the ball as it sinks into the rubber and makes contact with the wood part of the blade. As you do this drill, make note of what force contact feels and sounds like.

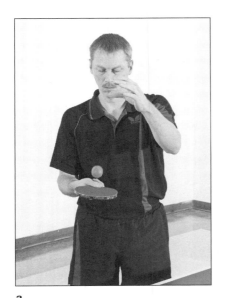  

a   *b*   *c*

Figure 1.11 Force contact, ball moving straight up: *(a)* hold racket with palm up; *(b)* bounce ball on racket as racket moves slightly up and down; *(c)* ball does not spin as it bounces.

Friction contact occurs when the racket brushes the ball off center, making the ball spin. You can experience this type of contact by slightly modifying the force contact drill. Begin as before, only this time, as your racket makes contact with the ball, move your racket to the left or right and brush the ball (figure 1.12). The ball will spin in the direction your racket was traveling at contact. As you touch the ball with friction contact, notice that the touch has a softer feel and makes a quieter sound than the force contact did.

Table tennis is a game of both great ball speed and spin. As your hand skills increase, you will learn how to touch a ball to produce the right blend of speed and spin required for each stroke.

When to Touch the Ball

There are three possible times to contact a ball, also referred to as *timing*: as the ball is still rising after it hits your side of the table, at the top of the bounce, or as the ball is descending (figure 1.13). In general, you can produce the most speed by contacting the ball at the top of the bounce and the most spin by contacting the ball on the descent. Take the ball on the rise when you are simply redirecting your opponent's speed back at him.

a   *b*   *c*

Figure 1.12 Friction contact, ball spinning in the direction the racket is moving at contact: *(a)* hold racket with palm up; *(b)* bounce ball on racket as racket moves left; *(c)* ball spins in direction racket was traveling.

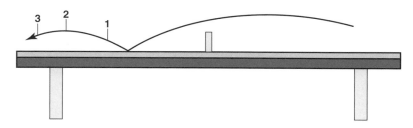

Figure 1.13 Path of the ball with three contact timings.

Where to Touch the Ball

This is the most important of the three basic elements. Where your racket touches the ball not only produces different spins but also controls the direction the ball will travel. To control the height of your returns, aim for one of three locations on the ball: above center, at center, and below center (figure 1.14).

Throughout this book, I will use these three basic elements to teach each new stroke. As you become accustomed to how these elements work together to control the ball, you will quickly learn to correct your own mistakes.

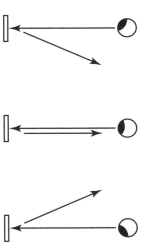

Figure 1.14 Three places of contact on the ball: above center, ball goes downward; at center, ball goes straight; below center, ball goes upward.

DEVELOPING HAND SKILLS

Table tennis is a sport that requires a unique mix of explosive power from the legs and fine motor skills in the hands. Working to develop the hand skills necessary for controlling the ball should be your main focus early in your training.

One key method used to develop these skills is to learn to feed balls using a method of training called *multiball drills*. Learning to feed balls to a practice partner not only will help you develop your own hand skills, but also will be a necessary skill for most of the drills featured in this book.

As the name suggests, multiball drills are performed with a large number of balls that are fed continuously by a feeder to the person doing a set drill. There is no replay of the ball. Because of this, practice balls of a lower quality will do nicely. Balls are fed until a certain number are hit or a set time period has elapsed.

Multiball drills have the following advantages:

- You can have more intense practice in a shorter amount of time.
- Because no time is wasted chasing balls, more strokes can be executed during practice.

- You can practice varied skills without a skilled training partner. Because the feeder does not need to move or return shots, she easily can duplicate much higher level returns.
- You can quickly increase aerobic and physical capacity. A feeder easily can overload the person executing the drill, forcing an increase in aerobic and physical capacity.
- One feeder can work with a number of people at the same time, varying the drill to suit each person.

The basic technique is simple. The feeder stands to the side of the table near the net (left side of table if the feeder is right-handed, right side of the table if the feeder is left-handed). A large container of balls is within easy reach of the feeder's free hand.

To feed a topspin return, the feeder first bounces the ball on the table using his free hand so the ball moves slightly backward. As the ball rises after the bounce, the feeder uses a short forehand stroke to make contact near the top of the ball. She swings forward and slightly up with the racket. With practice, a feeder can apply varying degrees of topspin to the ball by varying the racket angle (figure 1.15). If more power is needed, the ball can be thrown directly into the racket and not bounced first onto the table.

To impart underspin, the feeder repeats the sequence as for a topspin return but makes

contact with the bottom of the ball with an open racket (figure 1.16). Again, the feeder can adjust the racket angle and the amount of friction to produce the desired effects.

Use the multiball drill to learn to feed multiple balls and develop your own hand skills.

Figure 1.15 Feeder using a short forehand topspin stroke to make contact near the top of the ball.

Figure 1.16 Feeder using a forehand underspin stroke to make contact with the bottom of the ball.

Multiball Drill 1. *Learning to Feed Balls*

Use the basic ball-feeding technique described in the previous section to try the following simple drills. For each drill, feed 25 balls as described at a constant tempo. Try to keep the ball deep on the table and imagine that you are feeding balls to a practice partner. Record the number of successful balls fed out of 25 attempted.

1. Basic topspin feed: Alternate placing one ball on the right half and one ball on the left half of the table

2. Basic underspin feed: Alternate placing one ball on the right half and one ball on the left half of the table

3. Alternate between feeding one topspin and one underspin to one location on the table.

To Increase Difficulty

- Feed balls at an increased frequency (greater number of balls per minute).

Success Check

- Check to see whether you are feeding the balls at a consistent speed, and to the locations you are aiming for.

- Make sure you first bounce the ball on the table before striking it.

- Check to see whether you are feeding the balls at a consistent height. If not, make sure you are dropping the balls from a short distance above the table.

Feed 25 balls at a steady pace for each of the three feeding exercises. Record the number of successful feeds you are able to execute.

65 to 75 successful feeds = 10 points

55 to 64 successful feeds = 7 points

45 to 54 successful feeds = 5 points

35 to 44 successful feeds = 3 points

Your score ___

Multiball Drill 2. *Building Hand Speed*

Using the three feeding exercises described in multiball drill 1, try to feed the balls as fast as you can for one minute for each exercise. Your goal should be to feed as many balls as possible in one minute while still maintaining control over where you are placing the ball and the type of spin you are imparting.

Success Check

- When using your free hand to pick up the balls, try to pick up several at a time.
- Keep your strokes short and try to establish a consistent rhythm.

Record the number of successful feeds you are able to execute within one minute for each of the three drill patterns and add them together to get your score.

193 or more successful feeds = 10 points

165 to 192 successful feeds = 7 points

135 to 164 successful feeds = 5 points

105 to 134 successful feeds = 3 points

Your score ___

SUCCESS SUMMARY OF PREPARING TO PLAY

In this step, you learned how to hold a racket, get in the proper ready position, and develop your hand skills through ball-bouncing and ball-feeding exercises. You also learned the three basic elements of all strokes.

To see whether you are ready to move on to step 2, add up your scores for both the ball-bouncing and the feed drills. If you scored at least 22 points, you are ready for the next step. If not, you need more practice.

Ball Control Drill

   1. Ball Bouncing   ___ out of 10

Multiball Drills

   1. Learning to Feed Balls   ___ out of 10

   2. Building Hand Speed   ___ out of 10

Total   ___ *out of 30*

Now that you have developed your hand skills and have been introduced to the science of table tennis, it is time to move on to learning the fundamental strokes. The next step focuses on the forehand and backhand drive strokes.

Hitting Drive Strokes

This step covers forehand and backhand drive strokes, which are also called counterdrives. The word *drive* refers to an attacking stroke in which the ball is driven forward with power and only a slight amount of topspin. When done properly, the drive stroke has a low trajectory over the net. You should hear a distinct, loud, hollow sound when you make contact with the ball, as the ball is driven straight into the sponge. Drive strokes are used most often against an opponent's topspin return.

As explained in step 1 (page 7), in each of the steps that cover strokes, you will learn the three basic elements of each stroke.

Three Basic Elements for the Drive Stroke

How to touch the ball = force contact with minimal friction (spin)

When to touch the ball = at the top of the bounce

Where to touch the ball = slightly above the center of the ball against a topspin return

FOREHAND DRIVE

The forehand drive is the main hitting stroke of the game. In the modern game, the forehand drive is used most often against an opponent's topspin return and can be hit with varying degrees of power. Against fast-moving balls, use a shorter swing with less weight transfer to simply redirect your opponent's power back against him. Against a slower-moving return, use the lower body to generate more power.

The backswing starts from the basic ready position you learned in step 1 (page 6). As you see the ball coming to your forehand, move into the backswing position by rotating your hips to turn your upper body back (figure 2.1*a*). At the same time, straighten your forearm a little and transfer your weight to your right foot (if you are a right-handed player). At the end of the backswing, the racket should be a little below the level of the oncoming ball and pointing back.

Misstep

You hit the ball too late, after the bounce.

Correction

Be sure to get your racket back early. The racket should reach the backswing position before the oncoming ball bounces on your side of the table.

Figure 2.1   Forehand Drive

a

b

BACKSWING

1. Weight on back foot
2. Forearm opens up
3. Upper body turns
4. Racket head at 90-degree angle from table and forearm

CONTACT

1. Transfer weight from back foot to front foot
2. Turn hips
3. Rotate upper body back toward table
4. Snap forearm
5. Make contact with ball at top of bounce
6. Force contact, not friction contact

c

d

FOLLOW-THROUGH

1. Finish with weight on front foot
2. Racket finishes about head high in front of face
3. On hard drives, racket may finish on left side of body (right-handed player)

RECOVERY

1. Relax forearm and let it drop
2. Move feet back to ready position

As your opponent's return contacts your side of the table, begin the forward part of the swing by transferring your weight from your back foot to your front foot. Follow with your hips by rotating your upper body toward the ball. The more weight you transfer, the more power you will generate.

Contact the ball at the top of the bounce (figure 2.1*b*). The racket moves mostly forward and slightly up. Use force, not friction, contact. Just before contact, your forearm begins to snap forward and up to increase the racket speed, obtaining maximum acceleration on contact.

Accelerating the racket through the ball is very important for all strokes in table tennis. It is not how hard your racket is moving at contact that provides power to the ball, but how much your racket accelerates while the ball is on the racket, which transfers energy to the ball. Therefore, all racket swings should go from slow to fast. To accomplish this, the forearm must snap at contact. This is possible only if the arm is kept very loose and relaxed at all times.

Misstep

Your racket does not make solid contact with the ball. You hit toward the side of your racket and not toward its center (mis-hit).

Correction

You are swinging too fast before you contact the ball. Remember, the swing should go from slow to fast.

Misstep

You lack power in your strokes.

Correction

This often is caused by too much tension in your arm. Try to relax your forearm completely and focus on snapping it.

The racket continues through contact toward your target (where you want the ball to go). This is most often deep into the corners of the table or into your opponent's playing elbow. Finish with the racket in a saluting position about head-high (figure 2.1*c*). Complete the weight transfer with your weight on your front foot.

To direct the ball crosscourt, point your shoulders in that direction when you contact the ball (open stance; figure 2.2). To direct the ball down the line, turn sideways more so that your shoulders point down the line (closed stance; figure 2.3).

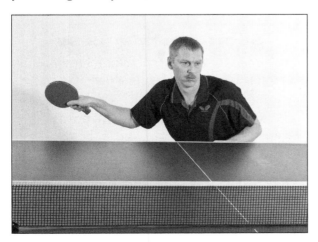

Figure 2.2 Body position for hitting the ball crosscourt (open stance).

Figure 2.3 Body position for hitting the ball down the line (closed stance).

Misstep

You have difficulty controlling the direction of your returns.

Correction

Be sure your shoulders are pointing in the direction you want the ball to go and try to have your racket travel in a straight line toward your target.

At the completion of the follow-through, recover to the ready position (figure 2.1*d*). Relax your forearm and let it drop down into the neutral position. Also, bring your feet back to the ready position. The entire swing should be continuous from the beginning of the backswing through ball contact, follow-through, and recovery.

Throughout the drive stroke, the wrist should be kept loose and relaxed. However, there is little use of the wrist when playing a controlled or even a medium-speed drive. Wrist snap is added to the full power version of the drive stroke, often called the *kill stroke*, which is described in step 9. When learning the drive strokes, focus on the forearm snap and not the use of the wrist.

Forehand Drive Drill 1. *One-Position Forehand Drives*

Have a practice partner feed 10 topspin balls to your forehand using the multiball feeding technique described in step 1 (page 9). Return all balls by using a forehand drive stroke. Return the first 10 topspin balls crosscourt and the next 10 down the line. For the final 10 topspin balls, alternate one return crosscourt and one return down the line.

At first, concentrate on controlling the ball by using mild racket acceleration only, snapping the forearm and using a little weight transfer. As you gain ball control, allow your weight to rock from your back foot onto your front foot to increase the power of your returns.

To Increase Difficulty

- Have your practice partner speed up the ball feeds.

Success Check

- Make sure that you contact the ball at the top of the bounce.
- Make sure that you contact the ball with force and produce only a light amount of topspin.
- Check to see that you are changing your stance from open to closed when changing the direction of your returns.
- Ask your practice partner for feedback regarding your technique.

Score Your Success

Earn 1 point for each successful return. Add up your totals for all three return locations to determine your final score.

25 to 30 successful returns = 10 points

20 to 24 successful returns = 5 points

15 to 19 successful returns = 1 point

Your score ___

Forehand Drive Drill 2. *Two-Position Forehand Drives*

The next step in learning to control your drive stroke is to learn to execute the stroke while moving into position. For this drill, have your practice partner continuously feed one topspin ball to the middle of your side of the table and then one to your wide forehand for a total of 30 balls (figure 2.4). Return all balls using only a forehand drive and moving from side to side. When moving, slide your feet side to side and do not cross your feet at any time. Return the first 10 balls crosscourt and the next 10 down the line. For the final 10 balls, alternate placing one return crosscourt and one down the line.

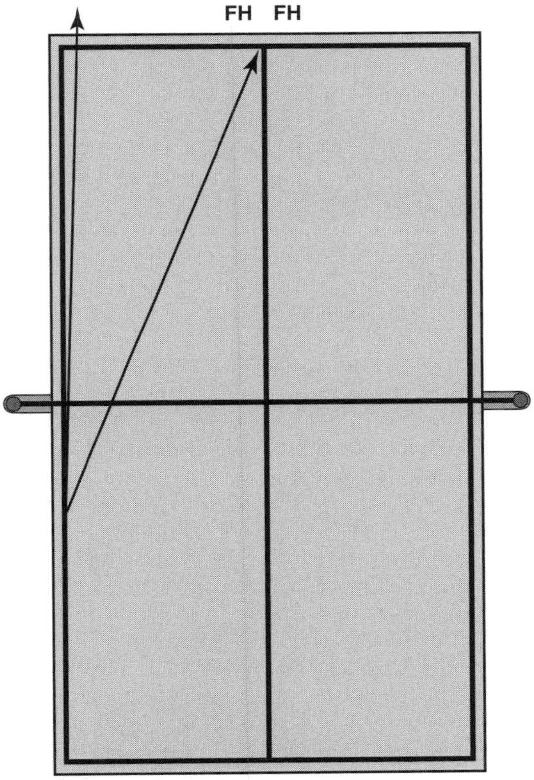

To Increase Difficulty

- Have your practice partner increase the angle of the placements to force you to move a greater distance.

To Decrease Difficulty

- Have your practice partner decrease the angle of the placements to reduce the amount you are moving.

Success Check

- Check to see that you are arriving into position to hit the ball before the ball bounces on your side of the table.
- Check to see that you are maintaining the correct form for the stroke.
- Ask your practice partner for feedback on your technique.

Score Your Success

Earn 1 point for each successful return. Add up your totals for all three return locations to determine your final score.

25 to 30 successful returns = 10 points

20 to 24 successful returns = 5 points

15 to 19 successful returns = 1 point

Your score ____

Figure 2.4 Feed placements for two-position forehand drives.

BACKHAND DRIVE

The sport of table tennis is very quick, and unlike tennis, there is not enough time to turn the body sideways to play both forehand and backhand strokes. Because of this, the backhand drive has developed into a shorter stroke than its forehand counterpart and is executed from a stance that allows a quick transition to the forehand stroke.

The backhand drive is executed from the same ready position as the forehand drive, with the right foot slightly behind the left (for right-handed players). The stroke is played directly in front of the body, so the backswing is short with the racket brought back until it almost touches the abdomen and with the racket head parallel to and close to the table (figure 2.5a).

Figure 2.5   Backhand Drive

a

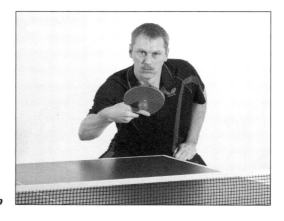
b

BACKSWING

1. Weight evenly balanced or slightly on left foot
2. Forearm closes, bringing racket close to abdomen
3. Racket head parallel to table
4. Short backswing

CONTACT

1. Make contact with ball at top of bounce
2. Force contact, not friction contact
3. Contact ball slightly above center
4. Forearm snaps up and forward, producing light topspin
5. Forearm pivots around elbow

c

d

FOLLOW-THROUGH

1. Short follow-through, traveling in straight line toward target
2. Racket finishes forward and slightly right of center of body

RECOVERY

1. Relax forearm and let it drop back to neutral position
2. Return to ready position

Misstep

Your backhand returns are inconsistent.

Correction

Make sure your forearm pivots around the elbow and the elbow does not lift up when you strike the ball.

As your opponent's return hits your side of the table, begin the forward swing with your racket, contacting the ball at the top of the bounce (figure 2.5b). The racket moves mostly forward and slightly upward through the ball, making force contact. The contact point is slightly above the center of the ball, and a small amount of topspin is imparted. At the moment of contact, the forearm snaps up and forward, pivoting around the elbow. Do not use wrist snap when trying to produce a slow to medium-speed return. Use the wrist only for the full kill stroke.

Misstep

You can't control the topspin on your backhand return.

Correction

Make sure your racket is moving forward and up when you contact the ball.

The follow-through is short and ends forward and slightly to the right of the center of the body (figure 2.5c). At the completion of the follow-through, simply relax your arm and allow it to drop down and back into the ready position (figure 2.5d). Always think of each stroke as unfinished until you return to the ready position.

Backhand Triangle

When playing backhand strokes, try visualizing the backhand triangle. Hold your racket 12 to 14 inches (30 to 36 cm) directly in front of the middle of your body. Imagine a triangle between the racket and your shoulders. When playing a backhand drive, you need to move your body to keep the ball within this triangle (figure 2.6). As you can see, you have a much smaller reach when playing backhand strokes than when playing forehand strokes. This makes it necessary to make many small foot movements to keep the ball inside this triangle. At the same time, where the triangle points when you contact the ball is where the return will go. Keeping the triangle concept in mind when playing backhand strokes will help you move to the ball better and help you learn to turn your body properly to control the direction of your returns.

a

b

Figure 2.6 Backhand triangle: *(a)* for crosscourt returns; *(b)* for down-the-line returns.

Misstep

You have poor directional control of the return.

Correction

Make sure your backhand triangle points where you want your return to go.

Backhand Speed

When learning to control the backhand drive, it helps to start with slow returns and build up the speed. A helpful technique is to think of this process like shifting the gears in a car. You need to start in first gear and work up.

The backhand drive (first gear) is a controlled stroke that uses only the rotation of the forearm with mild acceleration. The elbow of the playing arm stays close to the body, and there is no use of the wrist (figure 2.7a).

Second gear starts with the same basic stroke. When you make contact with the ball, push your elbow forward while your forearm rotates forward and up (figure 2.7b). This produces more racket acceleration and allows you to hit returns deeper into your opponent's court. Even though the wrist is still not used to add speed, you can hit quite hard in second gear.

Third gear is the full backhand kill. In this gear, the wrist is laid back toward the body during the backswing (figure 2.7c). The stroke is executed the same as in second gear, but during the racket's impact with the ball, the wrist snaps forward hard.

a   b   c

Figure 2.7 Three gears of backhand speed: *(a)* in first gear, the forearm rotates with mild acceleration; *(b)* in second gear, the elbow is pushed forward as the forearm rotates forward and up; *(c)* in third gear, the wrist is back toward the body during the backswing and then snaps forward hard at contact with the ball.

Misstep

You have trouble contacting the ball in the center of the racket, often missing the ball completely.

Correction

You are swinging too fast before you contact the ball. Remember, the swing should go from slow to fast.

Backhand Drive Drill 1. *One-Position Backhand in First Gear*

Have a practice partner feed 10 topspin balls to your backhand side, using the multiball technique. Return all balls by using a backhand drive stroke (first gear). Return the first 10 topspin balls crosscourt and the next 10 down the line. For the final 10 topspin balls, alternate one return crosscourt and one return down the line. Be sure to line up your body so that your backhand triangle points where you want the ball to go.

To Increase Difficulty

- Ask your practice partner to speed up the ball feeds.

Success Check

- Check to see that you are contacting the ball at the top of the bounce.

- Check to see that your racket is contacting the ball in the middle of the triangle formed by your racket and shoulders.
- Check to see that your forearm is rotating around your elbow.
- Ask your practice partner for feedback on your performance.

Score Your Success

Earn 1 point for each successful return. Add up your totals for all three return locations to determine your final score.

25 to 30 successful returns = 10 points

20 to 24 successful returns = 5 points

15 to 19 successful returns = 1 point

Your score ___

Backhand Drive Drill 2. *One-Position Backhand, First to Second Gear*

Again, have a practice partner steadily feed topspin balls to your backhand side using the multiball feeding method. Play the first return with a safe, controlled, first-gear backhand drive; then play the second return in second gear. Remember to push your elbow forward and increase your racket acceleration when moving to the faster second-gear return. Play 20 returns, hitting them all crosscourt.

To Increase Difficulty

- Ask your practice partner to speed up the ball feeds.

Success Check

- Check to see that there is a clear, visible difference in speed between your first-gear and second-gear returns.
- Ask your practice partner for feedback.

Score Your Success

16 to 20 successful crosscourt returns = 10 points

13 to 15 successful crosscourt returns = 5 points

10 to 12 successful crosscourt returns = 1 point

Your score ___

Backhand Drive Drill 3. *Combination Forehand and Backhand Drives*

Ask your practice partner to feed two balls to your backhand side and then two balls to your forehand side, for a total of 20 balls. Return all balls crosscourt using backhand and forehand drive strokes.

To Increase Difficulty

- Ask your practice partner to speed up the ball feeds.

Success Check

- Check to see that you are maintaining good directional control crosscourt with your returns.
- Ask your practice partner for feedback.

Score Your Success

16 to 20 successful crosscourt returns = 10 points

13 to 15 successful crosscourt returns = 5 points

10 to 12 successful crosscourt returns = 1 point

Your score ___

SUCCESS SUMMARY OF HITTING DRIVE STROKES

Drive strokes are used to return the ball with speed and minimum topspin of your own. The speed of your drive strokes depends on the length of the stroke you use along with the amount of body weight you transfer into the stroke. Against a fast-moving ball, these strokes are generally shorter and used to simply redirect the speed on the ball back against the opponent. Against slower-moving returns, a longer swing with more power is used to try to finish the point.

All drive strokes primarily use force contact, and to achieve maximum power, the ball should be contacted at the top of the bounce.

The drills in this step will help you learn to control both the speed and placement of forehand and backhand drive strokes. To see whether you are ready to move on to step 3, add up your drill scores. If you scored at least 35 points, you are ready for the next step. If not, you need more practice.

Forehand Drive Drills

1. One-Position Forehand Drives   ___ out of 10

2. Two-Position Forehand Drives   ___ out of 10

Backhand Drive Drills

1. One-Position Backhand in First Gear   ___ out of 10

2. One-Position Backhand, First to Second Gear   ___ out of 10

3. Combination Forehand and Backhand Drives   ___ out of 10

Total   *___ out of 50*

The drive stroke is the foundation on which all the rest of the strokes of the game are built. It is important that you gain good ball control with these strokes before proceeding to the next step, which focuses on understanding footwork and spin theory.

Understanding Spin and Footwork

Spin and footwork are two of the defining elements of table tennis. The small size of a table tennis table requires the application of spin to control the ball and keep it on the table. Your skill at both producing and controlling spin will, in large part, determine the level you can reach as a player.

The small size of the table also means that the incoming ball will reach you very quickly after your opponent strikes it. Because of this, table tennis has become a sport with very fast and explosive movements. To accomplish these movements, you need to develop well-organized footwork.

In this step, you will learn the basic concepts of spin theory as well as how to move quickly and efficiently around the court. The more spin you can learn to produce, the stronger your strokes will become. The better you can move around the table, the more opportunities you will have to play your strongest shots in a game.

SPIN THEORY

When you strike a ball off center, it spins. A spinning ball curves as it travels through the air because the spin creates greater air resistance on one side of the ball than on the other side. This forces the ball to move toward the area of lower resistance.

The greater the amount of spin applied to the ball, the greater the curve will be. By learning to control the amount of spin you apply to the ball, you can control the trajectory and the location of returns.

You must learn four basic types of spin to apply to the ball: topspin, backspin, sidespin, and no spin.

Topspin

Topspin is produced when the racket strikes the ball in an upward motion and the ball makes friction contact with the rubber. The swing starts from below the ball. In figure 3.1, the wheel attached to the table represents the ball. Imagine

Figure 3.1   Creating Topspin

1. Player starts swing from below ball (represented by wheel)
2. Racket travels upward, contacting wheel between 4 and 12 o'clock
3. Ball (wheel) spins in direction of travel

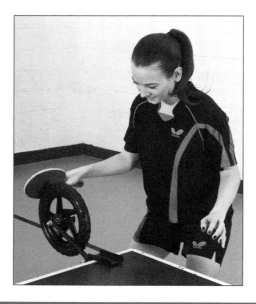

a clock face on the wheel. The racket travels up, making contact between 4 and 12 o'clock. Actual contact depends on the amount of spin to be added and the opponent's return.

A topspin return spins toward the direction in which it is traveling. As shown in figure 3.2, the ball has greater air resistance on the top and less on the bottom. This causes the ball to curve downward. When a topspin ball strikes the table, it jumps forward and stays low as shown in figure 3.3.

When a topspin ball strikes your racket, the spin forces the ball into a trajectory that is higher than normal. To control your opponent's topspin, contact the ball above its center with a closed racket (figure 3.4). The greater the topspin, the more closed your racket should be and the closer to the top of the ball you should aim.

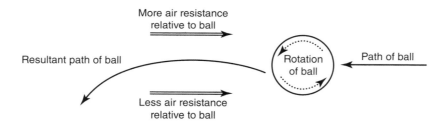

Figure 3.2 Ball rotation, direction of travel, and air resistance of a topspin return.

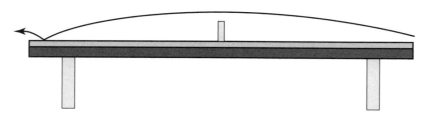

Figure 3.3 Flight path of a topspin return.

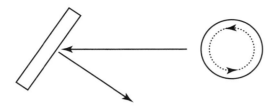

Figure 3.4 Controlling a topspin return.

Because topspin forces the ball downward and causes the ball to jump forward quickly after it contacts the table, players use topspin primary for attacking strokes. Through the use of topspin, you can control the ball while applying great speed.

Backspin

Backspin is imparted by striking the ball in a downward direction with friction contact. To accomplish this, the racket starts from a position higher than the ball (represented by the wheel in figure 3.5) and moves in a downward direction, contacting the ball between 3 and 6 o'clock, using a clock face as an example. Actual contact depends on the amount of spin to be added and the opponent's type of return.

| Figure 3.5 | Creating Backspin |

1. Player starts swing from above ball (represented by wheel)
2. Racket travels downward, contacting wheel between 3 and 6 o'clock
3. Ball (wheel) spins opposite to the direction of travel

A backspin return spins back toward you as it moves forward. As shown in figure 3.6, the ball has greater air resistance on the bottom and less on the top. This causes the ball to curve upward. When a backspin ball hits the table, the spin causes the ball to bounce up and stay close to the table (figure 3.7).

When a backspin return strikes your racket, the spin forces the ball into a trajectory that is lower than normal. To control your opponent's backspin, contact the ball below the center with an open racket (figure 3.8). The greater the backspin, the more open your racket should be and the closer to the bottom of the ball you should aim. Figure 3.8a shows what happens when a backspin ball strikes a neutral racket. The ball travels downward as it rebounds from the racket. Figure 3.8b shows the proper racket angle for hitting a backspin ball. The racket contacts the ball below its center, and the ball is safely returned to the other side of the net.

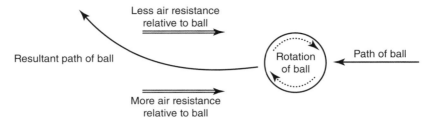

Figure 3.6 Ball rotation, direction of travel, and air resistance of a backspin return.

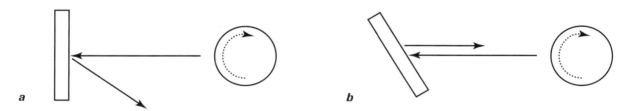

Figure 3.7 Flight path of a backspin return.

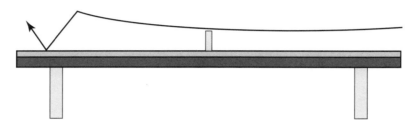

Figure 3.8 Controlling a backspin return: *(a)* backspin ball striking a neutral racket; *(b)* backspin ball striking an angled racket.

Players use backspin primarily for defensive strokes. The strong downward force of a backspin stroke makes it difficult for an opponent to attack and may force his return into the net. Because backspin returns rise when traveling through the air, backspin should not be used on fast returns because the ball will float long.

Sidespin

The two types of sidespin are right sidespin and left sidespin. Sidespin is most often used on the serve, but it can be used with any stroke. Because sidespin does not cause a ball to rise or fall, it is almost always used in addition to topspin or backspin.

A player produces right sidespin (figure 3.9) when the racket strikes the right side of the ball (figure 3.10). Right sidespin causes the ball to curve to the hitter's left while traveling through the air, but bounce to the right when it hits the opponent's racket.

Figure 3.9   Creating Right Sidespin

1. Player hits backhand serve with right side-spin

2. Racket contacts right side of ball (represented by wheel)

To return right sidespin, angle your racket to contact the ball on the left side of the ball (figure 3.11). Note that you are contacting the same side of the ball as your opponent did to produce the spin.

Left sidespin is produced when the racket strikes the left side of the ball (figure 3.12). The ball curves to the hitter's right while traveling though the air (figure 3.13), but bounces to the left when it strikes the opponent's racket.

Figure 3.11   Returning right sidespin.

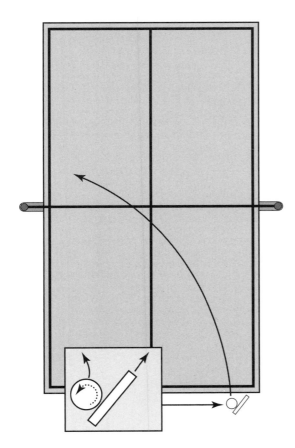

Figure 3.10   Brushing the ball on the right side causes the ball to turn to the left. The ball curves to the left as it travels through the air.

Figure 3.12　Creating Left Sidespin

1. Player executes left sidespin serve
2. Racket contacts left side of ball (represented by wheel)

To return left sidespin, angle your racket to contact the ball on the right side of the ball (figure 3.14). Note that, again, you are contacting the same side of the ball as your opponent did to produce the spin.

Sidespin makes the ball curve to the left or right, but does not provide any control of the height of the return over the net. Because of this, players almost always use sidespin in conjunction with topspin or backspin. Intermediate and advanced players sometimes add sidespin to their returns to create a larger angle and force their opponents to move a greater distance to reach the ball. The one stroke in which a large amount of sidespin is often used is the serve. Serves that use sidespin are covered in more detail in steps 5, 9, and 10.

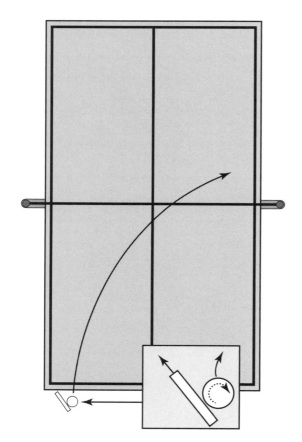

Figure 3.13 Brushing the ball on the left side causes the ball to turn to the right. The ball curves to the right as it travels through the air.

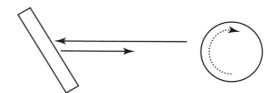

Figure 3.14 Returning left sidespin.

No Spin

No-spin returns are produced when a neutral racket contacts the middle of the ball and travels forward (figure 3.15). Hitting a ball so that it does not have spin is actually a difficult thing to do. A ball that has no spin to control its flight path tends to wobble unpredictably. Therefore, this type of return is difficult to control. No-spin balls are primarily used by defensive players or occasionally on serves.

Figure 3.15 Creating no spin.

To effectively return a no-spin ball, you need to make contact with the center of the ball and then execute whatever stroke you choose to use.

Spin Drill 1. *Backspin Over the Net and Return*

This is a great drill for developing hand skills (touch) and for learning to produce a lot of spin. Take a position on the left side of the table close to the net (figure 3.16a). Drop a ball on your side of the net. As the ball begins to descend, strike the bottom of the ball with a completely open racket in an upward motion (figure 3.16b). Your goal is to produce as much backspin as possible as you hit the ball over the net (figure 3.16c) and strike the opposite side of the table. After the ball strikes the table, the backspin should force the ball to bounce back toward you. With a little practice, the ball will actually bounce back over the net to your side of the table. Remember, you want to make as much friction contact as possible when contacting the ball. It will feel as though you are scooping the ball. Complete 10 repetitions.

Success Check

- Be sure to contact the bottom of the ball with an upward brushing motion.
- After bouncing on the opposite side of the table, the ball should begin to back up toward you.
- The faster the ball backs up toward you, the more spin you are producing.

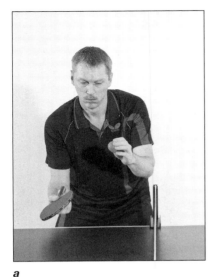

a

b

c

Figure 3.16 Backspin over the net and return drill: *(a)* position close to the net; *(b)* open racket as ball is struck close to the bottom; *(c)* ball returns backward toward the player.

Score Your Success

7 to 10 balls bounce back over the net = 10 points

5 or 6 balls bounce back over the net = 5 points

Fewer than 5 balls bounce back over the net = 1 point

Your score ___

Spin Drill 2. *Topspin Floor Bounce and Hit*

For this drill, move back from the end of the table approximately 5 feet (1.5 m) and assume a forehand ready position as shown in figure 3.17*a*. With your free hand, drop the ball from waist height. At the same time, drop the head of your racket by extending your arm and bending your right knee. Make sure to get the racket head low to the ground as shown in figure 3.17*b*. Now lift your racket almost straight up and try to brush the ball from low to high, making as much friction (spin) contact as possible (figure 3.17*c*). Your goal is to throw the ball high over the net so that it lands on the opposite side of the table. If you have im-

parted a good amount of topspin, you will notice a definite downward curve to your return (loop) and the ball will kick violently forward when it contacts the table. Complete 10 repetitions.

Success Check

- Check to see whether you are producing a looping (curved) return.
- Watch to see how much your return jumps forward on contact with the table. This will help you judge the amount of topspin you are producing.

a

b

c

Figure 3.17   Topspin floor bounce and hit drill: *(a)* starting position; *(b)* contact position with low racket and bent right knee; *(c)* follow-through position and the racket's direction of travel.

Spin Drill 3. *Right Sidespin*

Take a position on the right side of the table close to the net with your racket head facing down. Bounce a ball on your side of the net. As the ball begins to descend, strike the right side of the ball with the backhand side of your racket with the racket face pointing downward. Your goal is to produce as much right sidespin as possible as you hit the ball over the net. Your return should land around the middle of the table, kick to the left, and travel off the left side line of the table as shown in figure 3.18. Remember, you want to make as much friction contact as possible when contacting the ball. Complete 10 repetitions.

Success Check

- Check to see that your racket head is pointing down when it contacts the left side of the ball.
- Watch to see how much your return jumps to your right on contact with the table. This will help you judge the amount of sidespin you are producing.

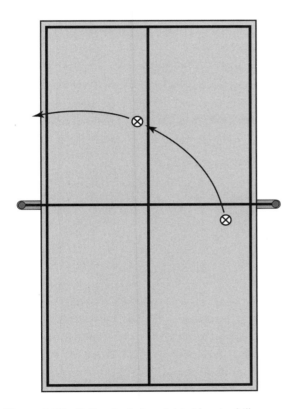

Figure 3.18 Ball path during right sidespin drill.

Spin Drill 4. *Left Sidespin*

Take a position on the left side of the table close to the net with your racket head facing downward. Bounce a ball on your side of the net. As the ball begins to descend, strike the left side of the ball with the forehand side of your racket with the racket face pointing downward. Your goal is to produce as much left sidespin as possible as you hit the ball over the net. Your return should land around the middle of the table, kick to the right, and travel off the right side line of the table as shown in figure 3.19. Remember, you want to make as much friction contact as possible when contacting the ball. Complete 10 repetitions.

Success Check

- Check to see that your racket head is pointing down when it contacts the right side of the ball.
- Watch to see how much your return jumps to your left on contact with the table. This will help you judge the amount of sidespin you are producing.

Score Your Success

7 to 10 balls go off the left side of the table after bouncing = 10 points

5 or 6 balls go off the left side of the table after bouncing = 5 points

Fewer than 5 balls go off the left side of the table after bouncing = 1 point

Your score ____

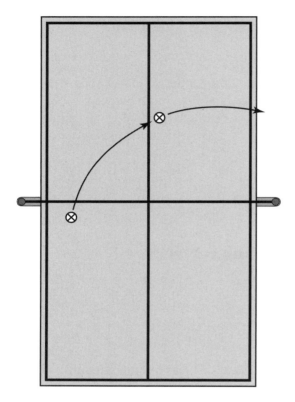

Figure 3.19 Ball path during left sidespin drill.

FOOTWORK

Between you and your opponent, there is only a 9-foot-long (2.7 m) table. With ball speeds that can reach more than 60 miles an hour (97 km/h), you have only a fraction of a second to judge the direction, speed, and amount of spin on your opponent's return; move into position; and execute your stroke. Getting into the correct position is not just a matter of foot speed but of knowing the correct steps to take to reach your desired position.

Before you learn how to move, you first must learn how to put your feet on the ground cor-

rectly. For quick movement, you want your body weight resting on the front part of your feet with your heels off the ground (figure 3.20). To accomplish this, imagine that you are making a fist out of your toes and your forefoot and then set that part of your foot on the ground.

By having all your weight on the front part of your feet, you increase the traction of your feet on the floor, which facilitates secure and quick movement.

Another key element to good movement is to keep your center of gravity low. As with a

Figure 3.20 Correct foot placement with the heel off the ground.

race car, the lower your center of gravity is, the quicker you will be able to turn and the better your balance will be. Your center of gravity is located around your navel. The easiest way to lower it is to take a wide stance with your feet—at least a little wider than shoulder width. Tall players should take an even wider stance.

Now that you know how to put your feet on the floor, let's look at the basic steps you need to learn to have a well-organized system of movement around the court.

Misstep

Your feet slip on the floor.

Correction

Make sure your weight is on the balls of your feet. This will increase your traction.

One Step

One-step movement (figure 3.21) is used to cover a short distance very quickly. Players most often use one-step footwork to return balls played close to the net and to quickly reach balls played back very fast by the opponent. As the sport has become increasingly faster, this is now the most-used type of movement.

To move to the right, start in the ready position and simply use your right foot to move to the ball, leaving your left foot in place (figure 3.22). To move to your left, move your left foot to

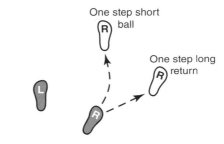

Figure 3.21 One-step movement.

the ball and leave your right foot in place (figure 3.23). After finishing your stroke, always try to return to the ready position.

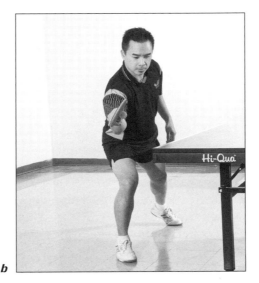

Figure 3.22 One-step movement to the right: *(a)* from ready position, push off with left leg; *(b)* take a wide step to the ball with right leg.

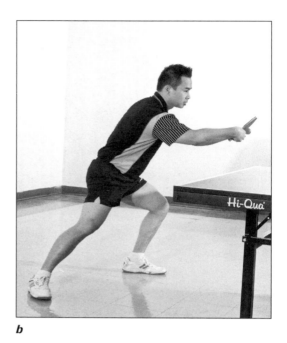

a　　　　　　　　　　　　　　　*b*

Figure 3.23　One-step movement to the left: *(a)* ready position; *(b)* move left foot to the ball.

The one-step movement allows quick movement into position and quick recovery to the ready position. However, the one-step movement can be used to cover only a short distance.

Also, because the second foot does not move into position, you will not be able to transfer your body weight to generate power on the ball.

Misstep

Your one-step movement puts you too close to the ball, making it difficult for you to take a full swing.

Correction

When moving your right foot to the ball, try to place it where you think the ball will bounce on your side of the table.

Side Step

The side step (figure 3.24) is used to cover short to medium distances, and it puts the body into position to generate powerful strokes. The side step should be used whenever possible to cover medium-length movements (3 to 6 feet, or 1 to 2 m). It can be used to move in either direction.

To move to your right using the side step, slide your left foot close to your right foot and then step to the ball using the right foot (figure 3.25). To move to your left, reverse the movement. At

Figure 3.24　Side step movement.

the end of the side step, your body should be back in the ready position. After executing your stroke, reverse your footwork to return to your original position.

Figure 3.25 **Side Step to the Right**

a

READY POSITION

1. Finish forehand stroke
2. Initiate move to right by pushing off with left leg

b

SLIDE LEFT FOOT

1. Slide left foot to right

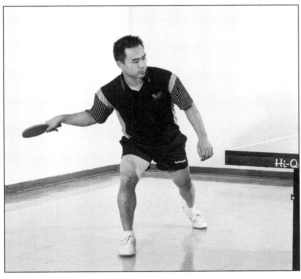

c

STEP WITH RIGHT FOOT

1. Step toward ball with right foot
2. Move into position to stroke ball

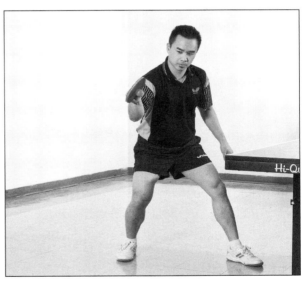

d

STROKE

1. Execute forehand stroke

Misstep

You are unable to transfer your body weight into your stroke.

Correction

Move both feet into position as often as possible. Take a one-step movement only when you do not have enough time to move both feet.

Misstep

You lose your balance when you move.

Correction

Take a wider stance to lower your center of gravity as you move.

The side step has been the primary form of footwork used in table tennis for many years. This type of footwork will put you in the best position to transfer your full weight into each stroke and develop maximum power and spin on your strokes. By moving both feet into proper position, you also maintain better balance and are able to recover quickly for your next stroke.

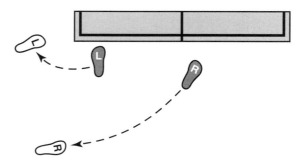

Figure 3.26 Pivot footwork.

Pivot

The pivot movement (figure 3.26) is used to pivot the body into the backhand corner and put the player in position to execute a forehand attack from the backhand corner. The movement always starts from the backhand ready position. It sometimes occurs after a side step move to the left (for a right-handed player). The pivot starts with the left foot taking a large step to the left, going completely outside the left side line of the table. The right foot then moves to the left so that, at the conclusion of the movement, the player is completely off the left side of the table and in position to execute a forehand stroke. This is a very quick movement, often more of a hop with both feet moving at the same time (figure 3.27). Note that both feet are pointing back toward the table. This is important because it puts the body into position to transfer your weight and power toward your target. If you are left handed, reverse these instructions.

Figure 3.27 | **Pivot Step**

READY POSITION

1. Start by pushing off with right foot
2. Take big step toward left with left foot
3. Step completely off left side of table

a

b

c

PIVOT STEP

1. Bring right foot back into position
2. Keep right foot behind left
3. Rotate upper body to play forehand

CONTACT

1. Play strong forehand drive
2. Body weight travels toward intended target
3. Recover by reversing movement and returning to ready position

Cross Step

The cross step (figure 3.28) is used to cover a large distance when moving to the forehand. It is frequently used by players who cover most of the table with their forehands and usually begins after the player has executed a forehand from the backhand corner.

Begin the cross step by taking a wide step with the right leg (if you are right-handed) (figure 3.29). Step across with the left leg in front of the right leg and strike the ball. At the end of the stroke, the right leg finishes in a wide position

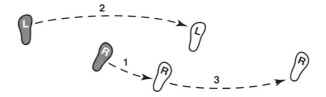

Figure 3.28   Cross step movement.

to allow you to push back to the left. If you are left-handed, reverse these instructions. This is the most advanced type of footwork and will be used more in later steps.

Figure 3.29   Cross Step

a

b

READY POSITION

1. In backhand corner as ball is directed to wide forehand

WIDE STEP

1. Take wide step to forehand

c

d

STEP ACROSS

1. Left leg crosses over
2. As left leg crosses, make contact with ball and execute forehand stroke

FOLLOW-THROUGH

1. Right leg finishes in wide position
2. Move back to the left

Misstep

You have difficulty recovering back into position after making a cross step.

Correction

Make sure to finish the movement by moving your right foot wide to your right (right-handed player). That will allow you to push back to your left and recover back into position.

The cross step allows you to cover a large distance and still produce a powerful stroke. It is used most often by players who have dominant forehands. It does require strong legs to execute this movement. Older players and those who play a more balanced blend of backhand and forehand strokes normally do not have to cover such large distances between strokes.

Footwork Drill 1. *Three-Position Forehand Drives*

Have your practice partner feed you topspin balls using the multiball method. The first ball should be directed into your backhand corner, the second ball to the middle of the table, and the third to your wide forehand (figure 3.30). After three balls, your partner should pause briefly to allow you to recover back into position to repeat the drill.

Return all balls using only your forehand drive. The target for your returns is the forehand side of your partner's table. The focus of this drill should be on using the proper side step movement. Have your practice partner feed you a total of 30 balls.

To Increase Difficulty

- Have your practice partner reduce the length of the pause between the third ball and the first ball of the next pattern.

Success Check

- Be sure to maintain your balance while moving.
- Check to see that you are using a side step and not a one-step movement.
- Ask your practice partner to evaluate and score your footwork.

Score Your Success

As you perform the drill, ask your practice partner to score your footwork on a scale of 1 (poor) to 10 (excellent).

Your score ___

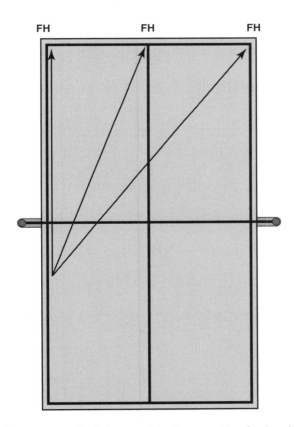

Figure 3.30 Ball placement for three-position forehand drives.

Footwork Drill 2. *Pivot Drill*

For this drill, have your practice partner send all balls to your backhand side. Execute two backhand drives; then, using the correct pivot footwork, move into your backhand corner and make two forehand drives. Move back into the ready position. Complete 10 pivot steps for a total of 40 balls.

To Increase Difficulty

- Have your practice partner increase the rate she is feeding the balls.

Success Check

- Make sure that when you pivot, your feet are pointing back toward the table.
- Be sure to take a large enough first step with your left foot to get completely outside the side line of the table.
- Ask your practice partner for feedback on your footwork.

Score Your Success

As you perform the drill, ask your practice partner to score your footwork on a scale of 1 (poor) to 10 (excellent).

Your score _____

Footwork Drill 3. *Falkenberg Drill*

This is one of the most popular drills worldwide. It is named after the Swedish table tennis club that popularized it. The Falkenberg drill combines both forehand and backhand drives along with pivot and side step movements.

This drill uses a three-ball pattern. Have your practice partner send two balls to your backhand side and then one ball to the middle of your forehand side. Use a backhand drive to return the first ball; then pivot into the backhand corner and return the second ball with a forehand drive (figure 3.31). Move to your forehand using a side step and return the third ball with another forehand drive. Repeat the pattern 10 times for a total of 30 balls. Your practice partner should pause briefly between the last ball of the pattern (the third ball) and the first ball of the next pattern to allow you time to recover back into the ready position.

To Increase Difficulty

- Have your practice partner reduce the pause time between patterns.

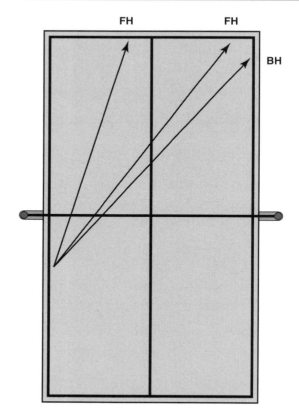

Figure 3.31 Ball placement for the Falkenberg drill.

Success Check

- Check that you are using a separate pivot movement and side step movement.
- Work on recovering to the ready position as quickly as possible after the third ball in the pattern.
- Ask your practice partner for feedback on your footwork.

Score Your Success

As you perform the drill, have your practice partner score your footwork on a scale of 1 (poor) to 10 (excellent).

Your score ____

Footwork Drill 4. *Falkenberg Drill With Cross Step*

This is the same as the Falkenberg drill, except that your training partner now places all the balls deep into the corners (figure 3.32). A side step

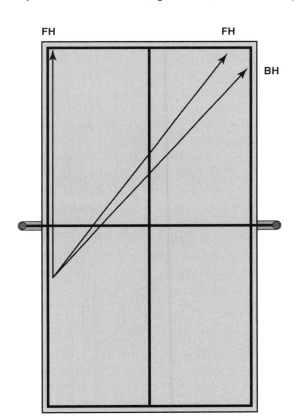

Figure 3.32 Ball placement for the Falkenberg drill with cross step.

will not allow you to move all the way from your backhand corner to reach a ball placed wide to your forehand. You will need to use the cross step. When you first attempt this drill, have your training partner slow down the pace on the ball until you feel comfortable with the movements.

Success Check

- Make sure you take the big first step with your right leg (right-handed player) when starting the cross step move to the wide forehand.
- Check to see that you are contacting the wide forehand just as the left leg crosses over the right and the leg is contacting the ground.
- Ask your practice partner to evaluate your footwork.

Score Your Success

As you perform the drill, have your practice partner score your footwork on a scale of 1 (poor) to 10 (excellent).

Your score _____

SUCCESS SUMMARY OF UNDERSTANDING SPIN AND FOOTWORK

In this step, you learned basic spin theory and proper footwork. Spin and footwork are the defining characteristics of table tennis, and understanding these concepts will allow you to progress quickly as a player.

The drills in this step will help you learn to produce spin and properly move to the ball. To see whether you are ready to move on to step 4, add up your drill scores. If you scored at least 60 points, you are ready for the next step. If not, you need more practice.

Spin Drills

1. Backspin Over the Net and Return   ___ out of 10

2. Topspin Floor Bounce and Hit   ___ out of 10

3. Right Sidespin   ___ out of 10

4. Left Sidespin   ___ out of 10

Footwork Drills

1. Three-Position Forehand Drives   ___ out of 10

2. Pivot Drill   ___ out of 10

3. Falkenberg Drill   ___ out of 10

4. Falkenberg Drill With Cross Step   ___ out of 10

Total   ___ *out of 80*

Now that you understand how to move to the ball and how spin theory applies to table tennis, we can move on to learning the spin strokes of the game. In step 4 you will learn the most popular and varied strokes in the game. All spin strokes are produced by contacting the ball with more friction than force. Spin is the defining element of the sport of table tennis. Controlling the ball by applying various types and amounts of spin is an exciting skill that is a great deal of fun to learn.

Executing Spin Strokes

The ability to apply a large amount of spin to your strokes is critical in table tennis. Step 3 introduced the basic theory of spin. In this step, you will learn the basic strokes used to produce that spin. These are the dominant strokes of the game and include the push stroke as well as topspin strokes against both backspin and topspin returns.

PUSH STROKE

The push stroke is a backspin stroke used against an opponent's backspin serve or return. It is the easiest way to return a backspin ball as you are going against (i.e., trying to stop) your opponent's spin. Because backspin makes the ball rise in the air during flight, you cannot add much speed to this stroke. For that reason, push strokes are mainly defensive and are used to place and control the ball. However, at beginning and even intermediate levels of play, you can win points with the push stroke by changing the amount of spin on your returns to force your opponent to make errors.

Three Basic Elements for the Push Stroke

How to touch the ball = with maximum friction

When to touch the ball = as the ball is descending

Where to touch the ball = toward the bottom of the ball

Misstep

You have difficulty controlling the placement of your push returns.

Correction

Make sure your racket is moving toward your target.

Backhand Push

Use the backhand push stroke against a long backspin return. The backhand push has a short backswing and is executed mainly with the use of the forearm. The wrist is used also to add varying amounts of backspin to the ball at contact.

When first learning this stroke, try to produce as much backspin as you can. Learning to brush the ball with your racket to produce heavy spin will help you control this stroke.

Starting from the ready position, move into a position that centers the ball in the backhand triangle as discussed in step 2 (page 19). Bring the racket back to the center of your body by rotating your forearm around your elbow (figure 4.1a). At the conclusion of the backswing, your racket should be in an open position, facing up. Your hips and shoulders should be rotated so that the right side of your body (if you are a right-handed player) is slightly closer to the table than the left side.

Figure 4.1   Backhand Push Stroke

BACKSWING

1. Bring racket back to center of body
2. Racket in open position to allow it to contact bottom of ball
3. Right shoulder and right hip are a little closer to table than left shoulder and hip

a

CONTACT

1. Forearm extends to bring racket to ball
2. Racket contacts ball as ball begins to descend from top of bounce
3. Point of contact with ball is fairly close to body
4. Racket contacts ball below ball's center
5. Wrist snaps forward at contact

b

FOLLOW-THROUGH

1. Racket continues toward intended target
2. Wrist snap adds more racket acceleration at contact
3. After stroke, player returns to ready position

c

Make contact with the ball as it begins to fall from the top of the bounce (figure 4.1b). Try to keep your body close to the ball so you need only a short swing to reach it. The more you have to extend your forearm to reach the ball, the harder it will be to control the return. At the moment of contact, you want your racket to brush the bottom of the ball (friction contact) to produce backspin on your return.

When first learning this stroke, mostly use only your forearm to accelerate the racket at contact. As you begin to gain control, allow your wrist to snap forward at contact to increase the amount of spin.

After contacting the ball, continue to extend your forearm forward. Finish the stroke with your racket pointing toward the target of your return (figure 4.1c). Throughout the stroke, the racket face stays open.

At the conclusion of the stroke, recover back into the ready position by bringing your elbow back into position to the side of your body and rotating your hips and shoulders back into position.

Short Backhand Push

The short backhand push is often used to return short backspin serves and drop shots. Although the stroke is the same as the backhand push, the footwork is different, and there is a greater need for a fast recovery back into the ready position.

For most balls placed short to your backhand, step forward with your right leg moving under the table (if you are a right-handed player) (figure 4.2a). If the ball is close to the left side line of the table, step in with your left leg, moving outside the table (figure 4.2b).

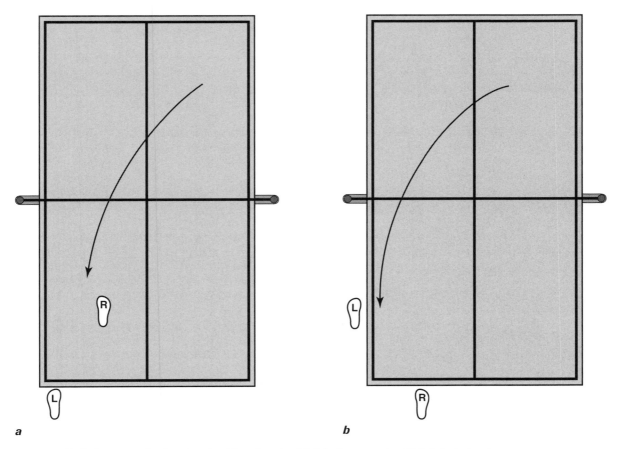

a   *b*

Figure 4.2   Ball placement for the short backhand push: *(a)* right foot step-in; *(b)* left foot step-in.

Misstep

You lose ball control when executing the short push stroke.

Correction

Keep your elbow close to your body and don't reach for the ball.

After executing a push against a short ball, your body will be over the table and in a very vulnerable position if your opponent makes a quick attacking stroke. It is important to make a very quick recovery back into your ready position. Push hard off your front foot and almost jump back into position (figure 4.3).

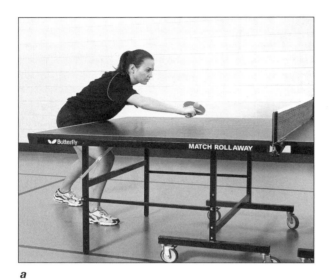

a

b

Figure 4.3 Recovery after a short backhand push: *(a)* the body is over the table after the stroke; *(b)* jump back to the ready position.

Push Stroke Drill 1. *One-Position Backhand Push*

Have your practice partner feed 20 backspin balls to your backhand using the multiball feeding technique described in step 1 (page 9). Return all balls crosscourt using a backhand push to your partner's backhand.

To Increase Difficulty

- Ask your practice partner to vary the amount of backspin on the balls he feeds you.

Success Check

- Make sure you contact the ball as it descends from the top of the bounce.

- Contact the ball below the ball's center.
- Ask your practice partner for feedback on your form and on the amount of backspin you produce on your returns.

Score Your Success

18 to 20 successful returns = 10 points

15 to 17 successful returns = 8 points

12 to 14 successful returns = 6 points

9 to 11 successful returns = 4 points

Fewer than 9 successful returns = 2 points

Your score ___

Push Stroke Drill 2. *Mixed Short and Long Backhand Pushes*

Have your practice partner feed 20 backspin balls, alternating between one ball short to your backhand and one ball long to your backhand. The feeder should use the multiball feeding technique described in step 1 (page 9). Return all balls crosscourt using a backhand push to your partner's backhand. Remember to use the proper footwork and, after making the short push, to recover quickly to be ready for the long push.

To Increase Difficulty

- Ask your practice partner to increase the frequency of the ball feed.

Success Check

- Check to see whether you are maintaining the correct form on your push strokes.
- Recover back to the ready position quickly after stepping in for the short ball.
- Ask your practice partner for feedback on your movement.

Score Your Success

18 to 20 successful returns = 10 points

15 to 17 successful returns = 8 points

12 to 14 successful returns = 6 points

9 to 11 successful returns = 4 points

Fewer than 9 successful returns = 2 points

Your score ___

Forehand Push

Like its backhand counterpart, the forehand push stroke has a short backswing and is executed mainly with the use of the forearm and the wrist. The forehand push is used most often against a short return because most players prefer to attack any long backspin balls to their forehand. Although not used a great deal at the upper levels of the game, the forehand push is an important technique for beginners to master. Other than in the backswing position, there is little technical difference between a backhand push and a forehand push.

Starting from the ready position, rotate your hips and shoulders so that the left side of your body is closer to the table than your right side (right-handed player) (figure 4.4a). The forearm pivots around the elbow so that the racket is moved into position in front of the right hip with the blade open and facing up.

Contact the ball as it begins to fall from the top of the bounce (figure 4.4b). Once again, try to keep your body close to the ball so you need only a short swing to reach it. The more you have to extend your forearm to reach the ball, the harder it will be to control the return. At the moment of contact, you want your racket to brush the bottom of the ball (friction contact) to produce backspin on your return.

As when learning the backhand push, at first use only your forearm to accelerate the racket at contact. As you gain control, allow your wrist to snap forward at contact to increase the amount of spin. Many players find it helpful to try to get their heads close to the ball at contact. This helps them remember not to reach for the ball.

After contacting the ball, your forearm should continue to extend forward with the stroke. Finish with your racket pointing toward the target of your return (figure 4.4c). Throughout the stroke, the racket face stays open.

As with the backhand push, you need to recover back into the ready position by bringing your elbow back into position so that the racket points straight ahead and your hips and shoulders have rotated back into position.

Figure 4.4   Forehand Push Stroke

BACKSWING

1. Upper body rotates so left hip and shoulder are closer to table than right hip and shoulder
2. Forearm rotates around elbow to bring racket close to right shoulder
3. Racket is open, facing upward

a

CONTACT

1. Upper body rotates toward ball, bringing racket to ball
2. Racket contacts ball as ball descends from top of bounce
3. Racket contacts ball below ball's center
4. Wrist snaps forward at contact

b

FOLLOW-THROUGH

1. Forearm extends toward intended target
2. Wrist snap adds to racket acceleration at contact
3. After the stroke, player returns to ready position

c

Misstep

You have trouble producing spin on your returns.

Correction

Create more acceleration by using your wrist at contact.

Short Forehand Push

The short forehand push against a short backspin return can be directed back to the opponent either short or long. Again, the only difference in the technique when pushing against a short return is the footwork.

For all short returns to your forehand, step in under the table with the right foot to reach the return (if you are a right-handed player) (figure 4.5).

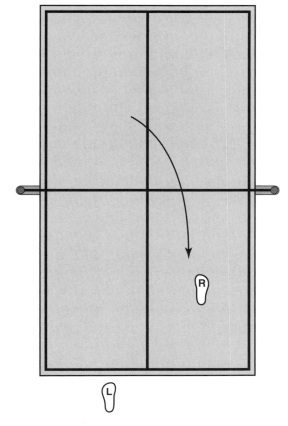

Figure 4.5 Ball placement for a right foot step-in during a short forehand push.

Misstep

The ball travels too high over the net.

Correction

You are contacting the ball too low, below the center of the ball. Try closing your racket face a little.

As with the short backhand push, when you finish this stroke you will be leaning over the table with your right foot well under it. You must make a fast recovery back into the ready position to be in position to defend against your opponent's attack or to initiate your own attack against a weak return. Push hard off your front foot and jump back into position (figure 4.6).

a   b

Figure 4.6 Recovery after a short forehand push: *(a)* the body is over the table and the right foot is under the table; *(b)* jump back to ready position.

Push Stroke Drill 3.   *One-Position Forehand Push*

Have your practice partner feed 20 backspin balls to your forehand using the multiball feeding technique described in step 1 (page 9). Return all balls crosscourt using a forehand push to your partner's forehand.

To Increase Difficulty

- Ask your practice partner to vary the amount of backspin on the returns.

Success Check

- Contact the ball as it descends from the top of the bounce.
- Be sure to contact the ball below the ball's center.

- Ask your practice partner for feedback on your form and on the amount of backspin you produce on your returns.

Score Your Success

18 to 20 successful returns = 10 points

15 to 17 successful returns = 8 points

12 to 14 successful returns = 6 points

9 to 11 successful returns = 4 points

Fewer than 9 successful returns = 2 points

Your score ___

Push Stroke Drill 4.   *Mixed Short and Long Forehand Pushes*

Have your practice partner feed 20 backspin balls, alternating between one ball short to your forehand and one ball long to your forehand. The feeder should use the multiball feeding technique described in step 1 (page 9). Return all balls

crosscourt using a forehand push to your partner's forehand. Remember to use the proper footwork and, after making the short push, to recover quickly to be ready for the long push.

To Increase Difficulty

- Ask your practice partner to increase the frequency of the feeds. This will force you to recover more quickly after returning the short ball.

Success Check

- Be sure to maintain the correct form on your push strokes.
- Recover to the ready position quickly after stepping in for the short ball.
- Ask your practice partner for feedback on your movement.

Score Your Success

18 to 20 successful returns = 10 points

15 to 17 successful returns = 8 points

12 to 14 successful returns = 6 points

9 to 11 successful returns = 4 points

Fewer than 9 successful returns = 2 points

Your score ___

Push Stroke Drill 5. *Figure Eights*

For this drill, have the feeder send you 20 backspin balls using the multiball technique, alternating one ball to your backhand and one to your forehand. For the first 10 balls, hit all down-the-line returns. For the next 10 balls, hit all crosscourt returns. You will need to use the side step footwork you practiced in step 3.

To Increase Difficulty

- Ask your practice partner to increase the frequency of the feeds.

To Decrease Difficulty

- Ask your practice partner to decrease the frequency of the feeds.

Success Check

- Be sure you maintain proper stroke technique.
- Check to make sure you use the proper side step movement.
- Direct your returns to the corners of the table.
- Ask your practice partner for feedback.

Score Your Success

18 to 20 successful returns = 10 points

15 to 17 successful returns = 8 points

12 to 14 successful returns = 6 points

9 to 11 successful returns = 4 points

Fewer than 9 successful returns = 2 points

Your score ___

TOPSPIN STROKES

The development of the topspin strokes closely parallels the development of the modern attacking game. The first use of a heavy topspin stroke came about as an effort to find a safe way to attack the backspin in defensive play, which was popular in the 1950s and early 1960s. By starting the stroke low and brushing almost straight up, it became possible to send a strong topspin return that went high over the net and violently kicked forward and downward after hitting the table. This made life very difficult for the chopping defender.

The high, looping trajectory of these early topspin strokes led to their often being called *loops*. As the years went by, players learned how to execute strong topspins against topspin returns (counterspins) as well. In today's game, topspin strokes and counterspins are the most-used strokes in the game. As discussed in step 3, topspin allows a player to hit the ball with great speed and still have it curve back down on the table.

Three Basic Elements for the Topspin Stroke Against Backspin

How to touch the ball = if a slow loop, with maximum friction; if a fast loop, with mixed friction and force contact

When to touch the ball = for maximum topspin, as the ball is descending; for fast topspin, at the top of the bounce

Where to touch the ball = if a slow loop, toward the bottom of the ball; if a fast loop, slightly below the center of the ball

When playing topspin strokes, you can contact the ball at several points along its path to produce varying amounts of spin and speed. For maximum spin, contact the ball as it descends. For fast topspin, play the ball at the top of the bounce.

Forehand Topspin Against Backspin

The forehand topspin is the easiest topspin stroke for a beginner to learn. The backspin return travels slowly, so you have more time to execute the stroke. Because you are adding to the spin on your opponent's return, you can produce the most topspin with this stroke.

When first learning this stroke, try to send the ball high over the net and create as much spin as you can. Adding speed to this stroke is easy. Developing the hand skills necessary for transferring all your energy into the ball as spin is the hard part to learn.

From the ready position with your left foot forward (if you are a right-handed player), bring the racket below the ball and slightly back (figure 4.8a). Rotate your hips and shoulders to the right and transfer your weight onto your right leg. The wrist points downward.

The Moving Face of the Ball

Always try to contact the ball on its face. The face is the part of the ball that faces the direction of travel, as shown in figure 4.7.

As you learn where to contact the ball for each topspin stroke, remember that the suggested contact point is on the face of the ball. For example, contacting the middle of the ball when it is on the rise requires a different racket angle than contacting the middle of the ball when it is falling.

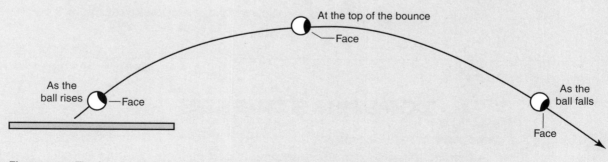

Figure 4.7   The face of the ball when rising, at the top of the bounce, and when falling.

Figure 4.8 **Forehand Topspin Stroke Against Backspin Return**

BACKSWING

1. Left foot forward (right-handed player)
2. Upper body rotates from waist to put weight on right leg
3. Right shoulder drops and is lower than left
4. Racket is lower than ball
5. Wrist points down

a

CONTACT

1. Racket moves in upward path
2. Racket contacts ball slightly below center of ball's face
3. Right leg straightens to transfer body's energy into ball
4. Forearm and wrist snap at contact to increase racket acceleration

b

FOLLOW-THROUGH

1. Weight fully transferred to left leg
2. High finish of racket indicates stroke was played for maximum topspin, not speed
3. Arm finishes in 90-degree position, indicating forearm fully snapped at contact
4. After stroke, player relaxes racket arm and recovers to ready position

c

Misstep

You have difficulty producing topspin.

Correction

Make maximum friction contact and create maximum acceleration when contacting the ball.

To produce a slow, heavy topspin return, your backswing should be very low and your racket should not travel behind your back because this will add sidespin. To get into this low position, bend your right knee and drop your right shoulder (right-handed player) (figure 4.8*b*). This will place all your weight on your right leg. This allows you to swing almost straight up and put all of your energy into producing topspin.

To produce a fast topspin return, your backswing should be below the ball, but also more backward so your wrist points back as well as down. Your right shoulder will still be lower than your left, but now it will also rotate more to your right (figure 4.9). This will allow you to swing both upward and forward to transfer your energy into producing both topspin and forward speed.

Figure 4.9　Backswing for Fast Topspin Return

1. Racket points back and down
2. Shoulders rotate back more than down
3. Weight transferred to right leg

Misstep

You lack speed during fast topspin returns.

Correction

Contact the ball at the top of the bounce with both friction and force contact. Transfer your weight at the moment of contact.

From the backswing position, push up with your right leg to begin to transfer your weight onto your left leg. At the same time, your hips, waist, and shoulders unwind to the left. The racket moves upward and makes contact below the center of the ball. At contact, your forearm and the wrist accelerate (snap up) to produce friction contact with the ball.

To produce a slower return with more spin, contact the ball as it is descending. To produce a faster return with less spin, contact the ball at the top of the bounce.

At the end of the stroke, your weight should have transferred onto your left leg. If you produced a slow, heavy topspin, your racket will finish about head high with your elbow at a 90-degree angle (figure 4.8c). If you produced a fast topspin, your racket will finish slightly more forward but with the elbow also at a 90-degree angle.

To recover to the neutral ready position, relax the biceps of your playing arm and allow it to drop back into position. At the same time, allow your weight to redistribute itself over both feet.

Topspin Drill 1. *Two-Position Forehand Topspin Against Backspin Feed*

For this drill, have your practice partner feed you 20 backspin balls using the multiball technique, alternating between one ball to the middle of the table and one ball to your forehand. Execute forehand topspin strokes, trying to create maximum spin, not speed. You can return the ball anywhere on the table. Remember to use proper side step footwork.

To Increase Difficulty

- Ask your practice partner to increase the frequency of the ball feeds.

To Decrease Difficulty

- Ask your practice partner to decrease the frequency of the ball feeds.

Success Check

- Contact the ball as it descends from the top of the bounce.
- Check to see that you produce maximum topspin.
- Use proper footwork.
- Ask your practice partner for feedback on the amount of topspin you produce.

Score Your Success

18 to 20 successful returns = 10 points

15 to 17 successful returns = 8 points

12 to 14 successful returns = 6 points

9 to 11 successful returns = 4 points

Fewer than 9 successful returns = 2 points

Your score ___

Topspin Drill 2. *Two Slow, One Fast Forehand Topspins Against Backspin Feed*

For this drill, have your practice partner feed 20 backspin balls to your forehand side using the multiball technique. Return all balls with forehand topspins. For the first two balls, play the ball as it descends and create maximum spin. For the third ball, play the ball at the top of the ball with more speed. Use the correct side step footwork.

To Increase Difficulty

- Ask your practice partner to increase the frequency of the ball feeds.

To Decrease Difficulty

- Ask your practice partner to decrease the frequency of the ball feeds.

Success Check

- Contact the ball as it descends to create maximum topspin or at the top of the bounce to generate more speed.
- Check to make sure you contact the ball with maximum friction on the first two returns and with a mix of friction and force on the third ball (fast loop).
- Ask your practice partner for feedback.

Score Your Success

18 to 20 successful returns = 10 points

15 to 17 successful returns = 8 points

12 to 14 successful returns = 6 points

9 to 11 successful returns = 4 points

Fewer than 9 successful returns = 2 points

Your score ___

Backhand Topspin Against a Backspin Return

The backhand topspin is used against backspin and is played in front of the body and not to the side like the forehand. Because of this, you will have less ability to transfer your weight into the stroke. For most players, this results in a less powerful stroke. The power for the backhand topspin comes mainly from the hips, waist, and forearm and the snap of the wrist. Higher-level players often change to a strong backhand grip to help produce more power when executing this stroke.

In the normal ready position, the left foot is slightly in front of the right (for a right-handed player) to allow for a quick transition to the forehand attack. The backhand topspin can be played from this position, but many players find it easier to play the stroke with the feet parallel to the table. Begin the backswing by deeply bending your knees to place the racket below knee height (figure 4.10a). At the same time, bend your wrist back. Also, during the backswing rotate your shoulders so the shoulder on your racket side is slightly closer to the table than the shoulder on your nonracket side.

Figure 4.10   Backhand Topspin Stroke

BACKSWING

1. Feet parallel to table
2. Racket side shoulder and hip rotated to be closer to table than nonracket side shoulder and hip
3. Bring racket below table between legs
4. Wrist laid back and down
5. Both knees bent, weight evenly distributed

a

CONTACT

1. Start stroke as knees straighten and hips and shoulders rotate to racket side
2. Racket travels forward and up
3. Racket contacts ball as it descends to produce maximum topspin
4. Wrist snaps up and forward

b

FOLLOW-THROUGH

1. Forearm and wrist snap up to provide maximum racket acceleration
2. Racket finishes head high and slightly to racket side of body
3. After stroke, player relaxes playing arm and recovers to ready position

c

Begin the stroke by straightening your knees and hips and rotating your shoulders to your racket side. At contact with the ball, the forearm rotates around the elbow and the wrist snaps up and forward to help impart the topspin to the ball (figure 4.10b). (Figure 4.11 shows contact being made by a player using his right hand.)

To produce a slower, heavier topspin stroke, contact the ball as it descends. To produce a fast topspin, contact the ball at the top of the bounce.

At the end of the stroke, the forearm will be fully extended and the racket will be about head high (figure 4.10c). The shoulders and hips will have rotated back toward the racket side. Circle your racket arm back into position as you recover into the ready position with the foot on your racket side back.

Figure 4.11 Player using his right hand as his racket hand, making contact during the backhand topspin stroke.

Topspin Drill 3. *Steady Backhand Topspin Against Backspin Feed*

For this drill, have your practice partner use the multiball technique to feed 20 backspin balls to your backhand. Execute backhand topspins, trying to create maximum spin, not speed. You can return the ball anywhere on the table.

To Increase Difficulty

- Ask your practice partner to increase the frequency of the ball feeds.

To Decrease Difficulty

- Ask your practice partner to decrease the frequency of the ball feeds.

Success Check

- Make sure your backswing places the racket well below the table and between your legs.

- Begin the forward swing by straightening your legs.
- Snap your forearm and wrist up as the racket contacts the ball.
- Ask your practice partner for feedback on the amount of topspin you produce.

Score Your Success

18 to 20 successful returns = 10 points

15 to 17 successful returns = 8 points

12 to 14 successful returns = 6 points

9 to 11 successful returns = 4 points

Fewer than 9 successful returns = 2 points

Your score ___

Topspin Drill 4. *Two Slow, One Fast Backhand Topspins Against Backspin Feed*

For this drill, have your practice partner use the multiball technique to feed 20 backspin balls to your backhand side. Return all balls with backhand topspins. For the first two balls, play the ball as it descends and create maximum spin. For the third ball, play the ball at the top of the ball with more speed.

To Increase Difficulty

- Ask your practice partner to increase the frequency of the ball feeds.

To Decrease Difficulty

- Ask your practice partner to decrease the frequency of the ball feeds.

Success Check

- Contact the ball as it descends to create maximum topspin. Contact the ball at the top of the bounce to generate more speed.
- Be sure to contact the ball with maximum friction on the first two returns and with a mix of friction and force on the third ball (fast loop).
- Ask your practice partner for feedback.

Score Your Success

18 to 20 successful returns = 10 points

15 to 17 successful returns = 8 points

12 to 14 successful returns = 6 points

9 to 11 successful returns = 4 points

Fewer than 9 successful returns = 2 points

Your score ___

Topspin Drill 5. *One Backhand, One Forehand Topspin*

For this drill, have your practice partner feed 20 backspin balls to your backhand side. Make one backhand topspin return; then pivot into your backhand corner and make one forehand topspin return. Alternate one backhand topspin return with one forehand topspin return for 20 balls. Use the proper pivot footwork you learned in step 3.

To Increase Difficulty

- Ask your practice partner to increase the frequency of the ball feeds.
- Alternate between slow and fast topspin returns.

To Decrease Difficulty

- Ask your practice partner to decrease the frequency of the ball feeds.

Success Check

- Maintain correct form on all returns.
- Use the correct pivot footwork.
- Ask your practice partner for feedback.

Score Your Success

18 to 20 successful returns = 10 points

15 to 17 successful returns = 8 points

12 to 14 successful returns = 6 points

9 to 11 successful returns = 4 points

Fewer than 9 successful returns = 2 points

Your score ___

COUNTERSPIN STROKE

Executing a topspin stroke against your opponent's topspin return is referred to as *counterspinning*. As you develop as a player, this stroke will take on more importance. At the professional level, this is the dominant stroke of the game.

The counterspin is a unique stroke in that it can be played both close to the table and away from the table to produce a wide range of returns with varying amounts of topspin and various speeds. If played away from the table as the ball is descending, heavy topspin can be produced. If played closer to the table, the ball can be played at the top of the bounce to produce very fast topspin returns. This stroke can even be executed off the bounce to place your opponent under great time pressure.

Three Basic Elements for the Counterspin Stroke

How to touch the ball = if the ball is descending, use more friction and less force contact; if the ball is at the top of the bounce, use equal force and friction contact; if the ball is rising, use mostly friction contact as you redirect the speed of the ball back to the opponent

When to touch the ball = if the ball is away from the table, hit it either at the top of the bounce or as it descends; if the ball is close to the table, hit it at the top of the bounce to create maximum speed or on the rise to redirect the speed of the ball back to your opponent

Where to touch the ball = if the ball is descending, contact it at the center of its face; if the ball is at the top of the bounce, contact it above the center of its face; if the ball is rising, contact it toward the top of its face

Forehand Counterspin

From a ready position with the foot on your nonracket side forward, transfer your weight to your racket-side leg by bending your knee and rotating your upper body to your racket side. Your racket should be back and lower than the oncoming ball (figure 4.12a). However, your racket does not need to be as low as it was when playing a topspin against a backspin return. Extend your forearm and lay back your wrist, holding the racket in a closed position.

Figure 4.12   **Forehand Counterspin Stroke**

BACKSWING

1. Foot on nonracket side forward
2. Upper body rotated to racket side
3. Weight on back foot
4. Forearm extended
5. Wrist laid back
6. Racket a little lower than oncoming ball

a

b

c

CONTACT

1. Transfer weight from racket-side leg to other leg
2. Rotate upper body to bring racket to ball
3. Contact ball at top of bounce (for maximum speed) with closed racket
4. Forearm and wrist snap at contact to increase racket acceleration

FOLLOW-THROUGH

1. Weight fully transferred to nonracket side leg
2. Upper body rotated to nonracket side
3. Forearm finishes at 90-degree position, indicating it snapped to add maximum acceleration
4. Racket finishes head high
5. After stroke, relax racket arm and recover to ready position

Misstep

You consistently hit the ball long off the table.

Correction

Adjust your contact position on the ball by aiming higher on the ball, using a more closed blade.

Begin the forward movement of the counterspin stroke by pushing off your racket-side leg and rotating your body back. Your racket will move forward and upward. Contact the ball with a closed racket above the center of the ball's face (figure 4.12*b*). (Figure 4.13 shows a player making contact using his right hand as his racket hand.) The more topspin your opponent puts on his return, the more toward the top of the ball you have to aim and the more closed your racket should be. Note that your swing is more horizontal than it was when executing a topspin against a backspin ball, and you should try to stroke toward your target.

Figure 4.13 Player using his right hand as his racket hand, making contact during the forehand counterspin stroke.

At the end of your stroke, your weight should have transferred onto your nonracket side leg. Your racket should finish about head high (figure 4.12c), and your elbow should finish at a 90-degree angle.

To recover to the neutral ready position, relax the biceps of your playing arm and allow it to drop back into position. At the same time, allow your hips and shoulders to rotate back into the ready position with your weight redistributed over both feet.

Counterspin Drill 1. *Two-Position Forehand Counterspin Away From the Table*

For this drill, have your practice partner use the multiball technique to feed one topspin ball to the middle of the table followed by one topspin ball to your forehand side. The feeder should move back from the normal position close to the net on the side of the table, almost to the end line (figure 4.14). This will allow him to take a longer swing to add a little more topspin and speed to the ball. You should take a position several feet back from the table, far enough back so you can contact the ball as it descends. Return all balls using good side step footwork and the forehand counterspin stroke.

To Increase Difficulty

- Ask your practice partner to increase the frequency of the ball feeds.

To Decrease Difficulty

- Ask your practice partner to decrease the frequency of the ball feeds.

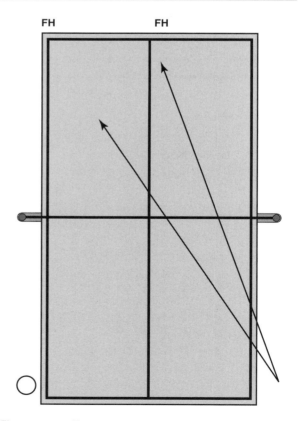

Figure 4.14 Two-position forehand counterspin away from the table.

Success Check

- Contact the ball as it descends.
- Contact the ball with a closed racket.
- Transfer your weight from your right foot to your left foot (if you are a right-handed player).
- Ask your practice partner for feedback about the quality of your topspin and your footwork.

Counterspin Drill 2. *In and Out Forehand Counterspins*

For this drill, have your practice partner use the multiball technique to feed 20 topspin balls to one spot on your forehand side. Start from a position close to the table and execute two forehand counterspins, trying to contact the ball at the top of the bounce. Then back up to middle distance and execute two forehand counterspins, contacting the ball as it descends. Repeat the pattern.

To Increase Difficulty

- Ask your practice partner to increase the frequency of the ball feeds.

To Decrease Difficulty

- Ask your practice partner to decrease the frequency of the ball feeds.

Success Check

- Make sure you successfully adjust your timing from the top of the bounce when you are close to the table. Let the ball descend when you are back from the table.
- Focus on producing more topspin when the ball is descending and more speed at the top of the bounce.
- Ask your practice partner for feedback.

Backhand Counterspin

Until recently, only players who used the shakehands grip were able to develop a strong backhand counterspin stroke. However, with the advent of the reverse pen-holder backhand, this advantage has been largely overcome. The backhand counterspin most often is played close to the table when the ball is on the rise. However, it can be played very effectively from mid-distance as well.

Often the backhand counterspin begins with the left foot forward (right-handed player) to enable a quick move to play the forehand. However, players with strong backhands may prefer to play this stroke with their feet parallel to the table. Begin the stroke by transferring your weight to the foot on your nonracket side and rotating your shoulders and hips to the nonracket side. Bring the racket back near the hip on your nonracket side, with the blade in a closed position (figure 4.15a).

Figure 4.15 Backhand Counterspin Stroke, Shake-Hands Grip

BACKSWING

1. Transfer weight to leg on nonracket side by bending knee
2. Bring racket close to hip on nonracket side
3. Closed racket position
4. Wrist laid back

a

CONTACT

1. Transfer weight to foot on racket side
2. Move racket forward and up
3. Contact ball in center of backhand triangle with closed racket
4. Contact ball on the rise to redirect the speed of the ball back to the opponent
5. At contact, forearm and wrist snap to produce maximum racket acceleration

b

FOLLOW-THROUGH

1. Arm continues to rotate around elbow to finish about shoulder height
2. Wrist in forward position at finish
3. Racket in closed position at finish
4. After stroke, relax racket hand and return to ready position

c

Misstep

The ball consistently does not clear the net.

Correction

Adjust your racket's contact position on the ball. Aim lower on the ball, using a more open blade.

To prepare for contact, transfer your weight from the foot on your nonracket side and rotate your hips and shoulder to your racket side. Contact the ball within the backhand triangle (figure 4.15b). (Figure 4.16 shows a player making contact while using his right hand as his racket hand.) For maximum power, contact the ball above the center of the ball's face at the top of the bounce with equal force and friction contact. If you play the ball as it is rising, contact the top of the ball's face with friction contact.

You can produce this stroke effectively using a pen-hold grip if you use the reverse side of your racket. The mechanics are the same as when using a shake-hands grip, except that when making contact with the ball, you must extend your elbow forward more toward the intended target (figure 4.17).

Figure 4.16 Player using his right hand as his racket hand, making contact during the backhand counterspin stroke with the shake-hands grip.

| Figure 4.17 | Backhand Counterspin Stroke, Pen-Hold Grip |

1. Pen-hold grip
2. Use reverse side of racket
3. At contact, focus on pushing forearm forward toward intended target

At the conclusion of the stroke, the racket should be at about shoulder height (figure 4.13c). Your weight should be on the foot on your racket side. To recover, allow your racket to circle to your racket side, bringing your elbow and racket back into the ready position. Quickly distribute your weight equally onto both feet.

Counterspin Drill 3.   *Backhand Counterspin Away From the Table*

For this drill, have your practice partner feed 20 topspin balls to your backhand. The feeder should move almost to the end line and add some extra topspin to the ball. You should take a position several feet from the table, far enough back so you can contact the ball as it descends. Return all balls using the backhand counterspin stroke. Direct the first two returns crosscourt and the next two down the line; then repeat. Remember to line up your backhand triangle so that it points to your target.

To Increase Difficulty

- Ask your practice partner to increase the frequency of the ball feeds.

To Decrease Difficulty

- Ask your practice partner to decrease the frequency of the ball feeds.

Success Check

- Start with the racket on your left hip in a closed position.
- Contact the ball in the center of the backhand triangle.
- Move your shoulders (backhand triangle) to control the direction of your returns.
- Make sure you produce a good amount of topspin by using friction contact.
- Ask your practice partner for feedback.

Score Your Success

18 to 20 successful returns = 10 points
15 to 17 successful returns = 8 points
12 to 14 successful returns = 6 points
9 to 11 successful returns = 4 points
Fewer than 9 successful returns = 2 points
Your score ___

Counterspin Drill 4.   *In and Out Backhand Counterspins*

For this drill, have your practice partner use the multiball technique to feed 20 topspin balls to one spot on your backhand side. Start from a position close to the table and execute two backhand counterspins, trying to contact the ball at the top of the bounce. Then back up to mid-distance and execute two backhand counterspins, contacting the ball as it descends. Repeat the sequence.

To Increase Difficulty

- Ask your practice partner to increase the frequency of the ball feeds.

To Decrease Difficulty

- Ask your practice partner to decrease the frequency of the ball feeds.

Success Check

- Make sure you successfully adjust your timing when hitting the ball at the top of the bounce when you are close to the table. Let the ball descend when you are back from the table.
- Focus on producing more topspin when the ball is descending and more speed at the top of the bounce.
- Ask your practice partner for feedback.

Score Your Success

18 to 20 successful returns = 10 points

15 to 17 successful returns = 8 points

12 to 14 successful returns = 6 points

9 to 11 successful returns = 4 points

Fewer than 9 successful returns = 2 points

Your score ___

Counterspin Drill 5. Two Backhands, Two Forehands Counterspin Pivot Drill

The feeder uses the multiball technique to feed steady topspin balls to your backhand. Execute two backhand counterspins; then, using good footwork, pivot into the backhand corner and execute two forehand counterspins. Repeat the pattern. Remember to use the correct pivot footwork.

To Increase Difficulty

- Ask your practice partner to increase the frequency of the ball feeds.
- Have your practice partner vary the amount of topspin on the balls he feeds you.

To Decrease Difficulty

- Ask your practice partner to decrease the frequency of the ball feeds.

Success Check

- Maintain correct form on all returns.
- Make sure you use the correct pivot footwork.
- Ask your practice partner for feedback.

Score Your Success

18 to 20 successful returns = 10 points

15 to 17 successful returns = 8 points

12 to 14 successful returns = 6 points

9 to 11 successful returns = 4 points

Fewer than 9 successful returns = 2 points

Your score ___

SUCCESS SUMMARY OF EXECUTING SPIN STROKES

This step introduced the basic spin strokes. Spin is the dominant element of table tennis, and the strokes you have learned in this chapter will give you the tools you need to develop your potential as a player.

The drills in this step will help you learn to produce spin and control the amount of spin and speed you add to the ball. To see whether you are ready to move on to step 5, add up your drill scores. If you scored at least 130 points, you are ready for the next step. If not, you need more practice.

Push Stroke Drills

1. One-Position Backhand Push — ___ out of 10
2. Mixed Short and Long Backhand Pushes — ___ out of 10
3. One-Position Forehand Push — ___ out of 10
4. Mixed Short and Long Forehand Pushes — ___ out of 10
5. Figure Eights — ___ out of 10

Topspin Drills

1. Two-Position Forehand Topspin Against Backspin Feed — ___ out of 10
2. Two Slow, One Fast Forehand Topspins Against Backspin Feed — ___ out of 10
3. Steady Backhand Topspin Against Backspin Feed — ___ out of 10
4. Two Slow, One Fast Backhand Topspins Against Backspin Feed — ___ out of 10
5. One Backhand, One Forehand Topspin — ___ out of 10

Counterspin Drills

1. Two-Position Forehand Counterspin Away From the Table — ___ out of 10
2. In and Out Forehand Counterspins — ___ out of 10
3. Backhand Counterspin Away From the Table — ___ out of 10
4. In and Out Backhand Counterspins — ___ out of 10
5. Two Backhands, Two Forehands Counterspin Pivot Drill — ___ out of 10

Total — ___ *out of 150*

You are on your way to mastering all the basic strokes of the game. However, actual points do not start with a stroke; they start with a serve or serve return. Step 5 focuses on the serve, perhaps the most important part of the game.

Serving

In all racket sports, the server has a huge advantage and should be able to win the majority of points on the serve. After all, the receiver does not know where the serve is going or what type of spin and speed the serve will have. This makes the serve and the serve return the two most important strokes in the game. No other strokes offer as many variations or are as complex. Recent rule changes mandate that the ball be visible to the receiver throughout the serve. This means that the server must remove his free arm from the area between the body and the table immediately after he tosses the ball so that the arm does not hide the ball from the receiver's view.

To become a good server, you must develop the fine motor skills needed for imparting heavy spin to the ball and for controlling the speed and placement of the serve. As your serving skills improve, you will find that these same hand skills carry over to lift other parts of your game. Serve practice should be part of every practice session.

In table tennis, the serve is used to force a return that allows the server to use her strongest stroke as quickly as possible within the point. Because most players have a stronger first attack with the forehand, most of the serves in the modern game are executed with the forehand from the backhand corner. This places the server in a position to use her forehand to attack almost any return. Backhand serves are more often used by players who have strong opening backhand attacks. At the intermediate and advanced levels of the game, players consistently change the amount and type of spin and the location of their serves to keep their opponents off balance.

Three Basic Elements for the Serve

How to touch the ball = varies depending on the type of serve being used; for maximum spin, brush the ball while making as much friction contact as possible; for more speed on the serve, mix friction contact with some force contact; the faster the serve, the more force is used

When to touch the ball = by rule, the serve must be thrown up at least 6 inches (15 cm) from the palm of the hand and struck as it is falling

Where to touch the ball = depends on the type of spin being put on the serve

The four components of the serve are spin, speed, location, and deception. This step focuses on spin, speed, and location. In step 10, you will learn how to disguise and use your serves in match play.

Serves are classified according to where they bounce on the receiver's side of the table. This step addresses how to execute these basic serves:

• *Short serves* are serves in which the first bounce on the receiver's side is close to the net. If unreturned, the ball would bounce several times before passing the end line of the table. Short serves are difficult to attack because the table is in the way of a full swing. Receivers often return short serves short to try to stop the server's first attack.

• *Mid-depth serves* are often called double-bounce serves. During these serves, the first bounce on the receiver's side lands about mid-distance on the table. If unreturned, the ball's second bounce would be very close to the end line. Mid-depth serves are often used to confuse an opponent. They are too long to be returned short but not long enough to be attacked easily.

• *Deep serves* normally are very fast and are directed to a corner of the table or into the opponent's body. They are very effective against a slow opponent and as a surprise tactic when an opponent expects a short serve.

UNDERSTANDING SERVES

All serves have elements in common. For example, when serving, you should always try to contact the ball as close to the table as possible. Contacting the ball high above the table creates a downward force that causes the ball to bounce higher on your opponent's side. By contacting the ball close to the table, the ball bounce will be lower and more difficult for your opponent to attack.

Learn to produce a variety of spins by contacting different parts of the ball when you serve.

When you contact the ball at any point off center, you create torque, or spin. You can also learn to read your opponent's serves by noticing which part of the ball he contacts.

Try to accelerate your racket on contact when you serve to produce maximum spin. Learn to use your forearm and wrist in a whiplike action to accelerate the racket as quickly as possible on contact with the ball.

Misstep
Your serve bounces too high on the table.
Correction
Contact the ball closer to table height.

Misstep
Your serves lack spin.
Correction
Make maximum friction contact and use a whiplike action of the forearm and wrist to produce maximum racket acceleration.

If you hold the racket with a shake-hands grip, change to a forehand serve grip when executing forehand serves. Grip your racket between your thumb and forefinger, holding the blade, not the handle (figure 5.1). The fingers should be completely off the racket and in a closed position. This type of grip allows for greater movement of the wrist, which aids in producing spin and in disguising the serve. After serving, simply open your bottom fingers and regrip the racket in the shake-hands grip to continue the point. Because the pen-hold grip already allows for full wrist movement, no grip change is needed.

Normally, forehand serves are executed from the backhand corner to set up a following forehand attack. Forehand serves are the most-used serves in the game. Typically, backhand serves are used as a change of pace from the forehand serve and to set up a following backhand attack. Backhand serves are executed with the normal shake-hands grip (figure 5.2).

For a serve to be legal, the ball must first bounce on your side of the table, travel over the net without touching the net or its supports, and land on the opponent's side of the table. To produce a deep, fast serve, the first bounce should be close to your end of the table (figure 5.3). For

Figure 5.2 Backhand serve grip.

a deep, fast serve, you need to use as much of the 9-foot (2.7 m) table as possible. Putting the first bounce as close as possible to your end line allows you to produce the maximum amount of speed and still safely land the ball on your opponent's side. For a short serve, the first bounce should be close to the net. The mid-depth serve should have a first bounce about the middle of the table.

Figure 5.1 Forehand serve grip.

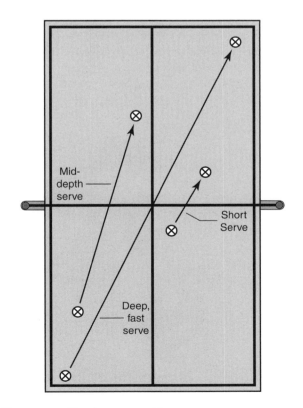

Figure 5.3 First-bounce positions.

Misstep

You have trouble controlling the placement of the serve.

Correction

Focus on finding the correct first-bounce location on your side of the table.

The rules of table tennis require that the server begin the serve by throwing the ball nearly vertically upward a minimum of 6 inches (15 cm) and striking the ball as it is falling. This makes the serve the only stroke in the game in which the ball is struck when it is falling straight down. This means that the face of the ball, where you want to contact the ball, is very low (figure 5.4).

Figure 5.4 The face of the ball is on the bottom as the ball descends.

SHORT SERVES

Normally, both forehand and backhand serves are executed from the backhand corner of the table. For all forehand serves, use the forehand serve grip and turn your body so your left shoulder and left foot (if you are a right-handed player) are forward. For backhand serves, use a normal shake-hands or pen-hold grip. Remember to remove your free hand from the space between your body and the net immediately after the toss when serving forehand. This is required by the rules for serving to ensure that the free arm does not block the receiver's view of the ball at any time during the serve. For backhand serves, your right shoulder and right foot will be forward, closer to the net.

Producing a good-quality short serve with a maximum amount of backspin requires the development of a lot of hand skills. Your racket needs to contact the bottom of the ball. As the ball travels straight down after the toss, move the racket below the ball and swing forward and upward to contact the face of the ball (figure 5.5).

a

b

Figure 5.5 Contact point for a short backspin serve: *(a)* forehand serve; *(b)* backhand serve.

The first bounce, on your side of the table, should be close to the net. The second bounce should land close to the net on the opponent's side. If left untouched, the serve should bounce three times or more before crossing the end line. A high-quality short backspin serve will actually begin to back up toward the net after the second bounce.

Forehand Short Backspin Serve

To execute a forehand short backspin serve (figure 5.6), take a position completely off to the left side of the table, so that your left hand is located at the left sideline (right-handed player). Your left foot should be in front of your right, and your upper body should be parallel to the left side line of the table. The racket hand and the free hand, which is holding the ball, are close together at the start of the serve.

From an open palm, toss the ball at least 6 inches (15 cm) high and, at the same time, rotate your upper body to the right, bringing your racket back into the ready position. The racket blade is open and the wrist is laid back. As the ball begins to descend, rotate your body back to the left and bring the racket to the ball. Contact the ball at the bottom of the ball's face with an open racket. The racket travels under the ball and up at the end. The follow-through is very short to help disguise the type and amount of spin on the serve.

The first bounce on your side of the table should be close to the net. The bounce on the opponent's side of the table also should be short. If done properly, this serve will bounce several times on the table or even back up toward the net. After serving, quickly get into the ready position to take advantage of any loose return.

Figure 5.6	Forehand Short Backspin Serve

a

b

BEGINNING POSITION

1. Stand outside left side line with left foot slightly in front
2. Upper body parallel to left side line
3. Serve grip, hands close together

BACKSWING

1. Throw ball up
2. Rotate upper body to right
3. Racket open in backswing position
4. Transfer weight to back foot

(continued)

Figure 5.6 (continued)

c

d

CONTACT

1. Transfer weight to front foot
2. Rotate upper body to left, bringing racket to ball
3. Low contact point on ball
4. Low position of ball to table
5. Forearm and wrist snap at contact to produce maximum racket acceleration

FOLLOW-THROUGH

1. Short follow-through
2. Upward motion of wrist

Backhand Short Backspin Serve

The backhand short backspin serve (figure 5.7) begins with the left shoulder close to the left side line of the table (right-handed player). Rotate the right shoulder and hip so they are close to the table. Both hands are close together with the racket behind the ball and close to the left forearm. Begin the serve by throwing the ball up as you rotate your upper body more to the left. This puts your body weight on your back foot. As the ball descends, transfer the weight to your front foot and rotate your upper body back to the right, bringing the racket to the ball. Contact the ball at the bottom of the ball's face with an open racket. The racket travels under the ball and up at the end. The follow-through is very short to help disguise the type and amount of spin on the serve.

The first bounce on your side of the table should be close to the net. The bounce on the opponent's side of the table also should be short. If done properly, this serve will bounce several times on the table or even back up toward the net. After serving, quickly get into the ready position to take advantage of any loose return.

Figure 5.7   Backhand Short Backspin Serve

a

b

BEGINNING POSITION

1. Right foot in front of left
2. Body rotated so right shoulder and hip are close to table
3. Racket behind free hand, which holds the ball, and close to left forearm
4. Shake-hands grip

BACKSWING

1. Throw ball up
2. Rotate upper body to left
3. Racket in backswing position and open
4. Transfer weight to back foot

c

d

CONTACT

1. Transfer weight to front foot
2. Rotate upper body to right, bringing racket to ball
3. Low contact point on ball
4. Low position of ball to table
5. Forearm and wrist snap at contact to produce maximum racket acceleration

FOLLOW-THROUGH

1. Short follow-through
2. Upward motion of wrist

Short Serve Drill 1. *Short Backspin Serve*

Using correct short serve technique, execute 20 forehand and 20 backhand backspin serves so that they bounce a minimum of three times before crossing the end line of your opponent's side of the table. If you can produce enough backspin, your serves will actually back up after striking your opponent's side of the table.

To Increase Difficulty

• Score only the balls that back up toward the net when the serve lands on the opponent's side of the table.

Success Check

• Contact the ball at the bottom of the ball's face with an upward racket motion.
• Contact the ball low to the table.

• Check the amount of backspin on your serves by observing the action of the ball when it lands on the opponent's side of the table.

Score Your Success

17 to 20 successful forehand serves = 10 points

13 to 16 successful forehand serves = 5 points

9 to 12 successful forehand serves = 1 point

17 to 20 successful backhand serves = 10 points

13 to 16 successful backhand serves = 5 points

9 to 12 successful backhand serves = 1 point

Your score ___

Short Serve Drill 2. *Ball Placement*

Place two standard-size sheets of paper lengthwise on the table, 1 foot (30 cm) from the net, so that one touches the right side line of the table and one touches the left side line. Serve 10 short forehand and 10 short backhand backspin serves to each target. For the serve to be successful, the ball must land on the target and bounce at least three times before going off the end line of the table.

Success Check

• Use proper serve technique for short forehand and short backhand serves.
• Make sure the ball lands on the target and bounces at least three times before going over the end line.

Score Your Success

17 to 20 successful forehand serves = 10 points

13 to 16 successful forehand serves = 5 points

9 to 12 successful forehand serves = 1 point

17 to 20 successful backhand serves = 10 points

13 to 16 successful backhand serves = 5 points

9 to 12 successful backhand serves = 1 point

Your score ___

MID-DEPTH SERVES

Whereas short serves are used to try to stop an opponent's attack, mid-depth serves are used to force your own attack. As the name suggests, these serves have a first bounce on the opponent's side that lands around the middle of the table. On the second bounce, the ball would land around the opponent's end line. This serve is both too long to easily be returned back short, but not long enough to easily be attacked. Often, the result is a weak serve return that allows the server to attack first.

Although the mid-depth serve can be produced using either backspin or topspin, the addition of sidespin makes this serve even more effective. Against a sidespin serve, the receiver has to deal not only with the uncomfortable mid-distance of the serve but also the fact that the ball jumps sideways on contact with the table. This serve is also very effective when directed toward the white center line on your opponent's side of the table. A serve that curves sideways across the center line can confuse an opponent as to whether to use a backhand or forehand return and force a weak return that you can attack.

Mid-Depth Left Sidespin Serve

The mid-depth left sidespin serve is the most widely used serve in competition. Often the left sidespin forces the receiver to return the ball to the server's backhand side, where the server is waiting to attack with the forehand. The mechanics of this serve are similar to those of the short backspin serve, except that you contact the left side of the ball (figure 5.8) and the first bounce is around the middle of your side of the table.

This serve bounces around the middle of your opponent's side of the table and then curves sharply to your right. If your racket is open at contact, the serve will have both sidespin and backspin. If your racket is closed at contact, the serve will have sidespin and topspin.

a *b*

Figure 5.8 Contact point for mid-depth left sidespin serves: *(a)* forehand serve; *(b)* backhand serve.

Forehand Mid-Depth Left Sidespin Serve

To execute a forehand mid-depth left sidespin serve (figure 5.9), take a position completely off to the left side of the table so that your left hand is located at the left side line of the table (right-handed player). Be sure to use the serve grip. Your left foot should be in front of the right, and your upper body should be parallel to the left side line of the table. Your racket hand and your free hand, which is holding the ball, are close together at the start of the serve.

From an open palm, toss the ball at least 6 inches (15 cm) high and, at the same time, rotate your upper body to the right, bringing your racket back into the ready position. Immediately after the toss, remove your free hand from the area between your body and the table so that the ball is visible to your opponent throughout the serve.

As the ball begins to descend, rotate your body back to the left and bring the racket to the ball. Contact the ball on the left side, the side closest to you. To accomplish this point of contact, you need to drop the head of your racket so that it points down. The arm swing is close to your body and resembles the swinging arm of a grandfather clock. Because of this, this serve is often referred to as a *pendulum serve*. At contact, snap the forearm and wrist to add to the racket acceleration. Use mostly friction contact because you are trying to produce varying amounts of spin, not speed. If your racket face is open at contact, you also will add some backspin to the serve. If your racket face is closed at contact, you also will add some topspin to the serve.

When following through, you can move the racket in the opposite direction to hide the point of contact from your opponent. The first bounce on your side of the table should be at about the middle of the table. This will produce a mid-depth serve on the opponent's side. After serving, quickly get into the ready position to take advantage of any loose return.

Figure 5.9   Forehand Mid-Depth Left Sidespin Serve

a

b

BEGINNING POSITION

1. Stand outside left side line
2. Left foot slightly in front
3. Upper body parallel to left side line
4. Serve grip
5. Hands close together

BACKSWING

1. Throw ball up
2. Rotate upper body to right
3. Racket in backswing position
4. Transfer weight to back foot

CONTACT

1. Transfer weight to front foot
2. Rotate upper body to left, bringing racket to ball
3. Remove free arm from area between body and table to allow receiver to see ball
4. Pivot forearm around elbow to allow racket to contact left side of ball (pendulum swing)
5. Snap forearm and wrist at contact to produce maximum racket acceleration

c

Backhand Mid-Depth Left Sidespin Serve

To execute the mid-depth left sidespin serve with your backhand (figure 5.10), begin in the same starting position as when executing a short backhand serve. Use a normal shake-hands or pen-hold grip. Your left shoulder should be about even with the left side line of the table, and your right shoulder and hip are rotated so they are close to the table (right-handed player). Your right foot is a little in front of the left. Both hands are close together with the racket behind the ball and close to the left forearm. Begin the serve by throwing the ball up. At the same time, rotate your upper body more to the left and shift your weight to your left foot. As required by ITTF rules, the free arm must be removed immediately from the space between the body and the table, so as not to block the opponent's vision of the ball.

As the ball descends, begin to transfer your weight to your right foot and rotate your upper body back to the right, bringing the racket to the ball. Contact the ball on the left side with the racket head pointing up. If the racket face is open, backspin will be added to the serve. If the racket face is closed, topspin will be added. On contact with the ball, the forearm and wrist snap to increase the racket's acceleration. Contact is mostly friction because you are trying to produce varying amounts of spin, not speed.

When following through, move the racket in the opposite direction to hide the point of contact from your opponent. The first bounce on your side of the table should be at about the middle of the table. This will produce a mid-depth serve on the opponent's side. After serving, quickly get into the ready position to take advantage of any loose return.

Figure 5.10   Backhand Mid-Depth Left Sidespin Serve

a

b

BEGINNING POSITION

1. Right foot in front of left
2. Body rotated so right shoulder and hip are close to table
3. Racket is behind free hand, which holds ball, and close to left forearm
4. Use standard shake-hands grip

BACKSWING

1. Throw ball up
2. Rotate upper body to left
3. Remove free arm from space between body and table to allow opponent to see ball
4. Racket open and in backswing position
5. Transfer weight to back foot

c

d

CONTACT

1. Transfer weight to right foot
2. Rotate upper body to right, bringing racket to ball
3. Contact ball on left side
4. Racket head points up
5. Snap forearm and wrist at contact to increase racket acceleration

FOLLOW-THROUGH

1. After contact, move racket in opposite direction (to right) to disguise point of contact
2. Recover quickly to ready position

Mid-Depth Right Sidespin Serve

To execute this serve, your racket should contact the right side of the ball (figure 5.11). The ball will break to your left when it contacts your opponent's side of the table.

The first bounce should be at around the middle of your side of table. The second bounce should be at the middle of your opponent's side. If your racket face is open at contact, the serve will have both sidespin and backspin. If the racket face is closed, the serve will have sidespin and topspin.

Forehand Mid-Depth Right Sidespin Serve

The forehand mid-depth right sidespin serve (figure 5.12) starts from the same ready position as that of the forehand mid-depth left sidespin serve. The only difference is that the racket contacts the right side of the ball instead of the left. To accomplish this, after the ball toss, bend your racket hand toward your body by breaking your wrist to the left (toward your body).

At contact, snap your wrist back to the right, away from your body. If you usually use a shake-hands grip, make sure you use the serve grip. Using the grandfather clock analogy, the pendulum arm will be moving away from you on contact. At contact, snap the forearm and wrist to add to the racket acceleration. Use mostly friction contact because you are trying to produce varying amounts of spin, not speed. An open racket face at contact also will add some backspin to the serve. A closed racket face at contact will add some topspin.

When following through, move the racket in the opposite direction to hide the point of contact from your opponent. The first bounce on your side of the table should be at about the middle of the table. This will produce a mid-depth serve on the opponent's side. After serving, quickly get into the ready position to take advantage of any loose return.

a

b

Figure 5.11 Contact point for mid-depth right sidespin serves: *(a)* forehand serve; *(b)* backhand serve.

Figure 5.12 | Forehand Mid-Depth Right Sidespin Serve

a

BEGINNING POSITION

1. Stand outside left side line
2. Left foot slightly in front
3. Upper body parallel to left side line
4. Serve grip

b

BACKSWING

1. Throw ball up
2. Rotate upper body to right
3. Break wrist toward body
4. Racket head points toward body
5. Transfer weight to back foot

c

CONTACT

1. Transfer weight to front foot
2. Rotate upper body to left, bringing racket to ball
3. Remove free arm from area between body and table
4. Forearm and wrist swing back to right to allow racket to contact right side of ball (pendulum swing)
5. Snap forearm and wrist at contact to produce maximum racket acceleration

d

FOLLOW-THROUGH

1. After contact, move racket to disguise point of contact
2. Recover quickly to ready position

Backhand Mid-Depth Right Sidespin Serve

The backhand mid-depth right sidespin serve (figure 5.13) begins exactly like the backhand mid-depth left sidespin serve. The only difference is that the racket contacts the right side of the ball. To accomplish this, the racket head must point down at contact. At contact, the forearm and wrist snap to produce maximum racket acceleration. Use a standard shake-hands or pen-hold grip. Remember to remove your free arm from between your body and the table so the ball is visible to your opponent. If your racket is open at contact, you will add backspin to your sidespin. If it is closed, you will add topspin. Use mostly friction contact because you are trying to produce varying amounts of spin, not speed.

When following through, move the racket in the opposite direction to hide the point of contact from your opponent. The first bounce on your side of the table should be at about the middle of the table. This will produce a mid-depth serve on the opponent's side. After serving, quickly get into a ready position to take advantage of any loose return.

| Figure 5.13 | Backhand Mid-Depth Right Sidespin Serve |

a

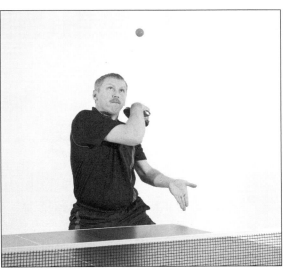

b

BEGINNING POSITION

1. Right foot in front of left
2. Body rotated so right shoulder and hip are close to table
3. Racket behind free hand, which holds ball, and close to left forearm
4. Standard shake-hands grip

BACKSWING

1. Throw ball up
2. Rotate upper body to left
3. Remove free arm from space between body and table to allow opponent to see ball
4. Racket head points down
5. Open racket face
6. Transfer weight to back foot

(continued)

Figure 5.13 *(continued)*

c

d

CONTACT

1. Transfer weight to right foot
2. Rotate upper body, bringing racket to ball
3. Contact ball on right side
4. Racket head points down
5. Snap forearm and wrist at contact to increase racket acceleration

FOLLOW-THROUGH

1. After contact, move racket in opposite direction (to right) to disguise point of contact
2. Quickly recover to ready position

Mid-Depth Serve Drill 1. *Mid-Depth Left Sidespin Serve*

Set a target on the right side line on your opponent's side of the table, halfway between the net and the end line. A water bottle or a soda can works fine. Your goal is to execute 20 forehand and 20 backhand left sidespin serves so they first bounce on your opponent's side to the left of the target and then break to your right and go off the side of the table in front of the target (figure 5.14). When practicing this serve, try to create as much sidespin as possible.

To Increase Difficulty

• Move your target away from the side line.

Success Check

• Contact the left side of the ball.
• The racket head should point down when contacting the ball during the forehand serve and point up when contacting the ball during the backhand serve.
• Watch the curved path of the ball to judge how much spin you are producing.

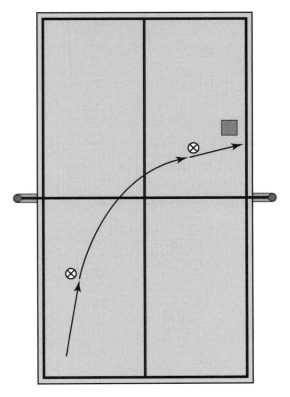

Score Your Success

17 to 20 successful forehand serves = 10 points

13 to 16 successful forehand serves = 5 points

9 to 12 successful forehand serves = 1 point

Your score ___

17 to 20 successful backhand serves = 10 points

13 to 16 successful backhand serves = 5 points

9 to 12 successful backhand serves = 1 point

Your score ___

Figure 5.14 Path of the ball during the mid-depth left sidespin serve drill.

Mid-Depth Serve Drill 2. Mid-Depth Right Sidespin Serve

Move the target from the previous drill to the same location but on the left side line. Execute 20 forehand and 20 backhand right sidespin serves so that they touch the table to the right of the target, curve to the left, and go off the side of the table in front of the target (figure 5.15). Once again, try to create as much sidespin as possible when practicing this serve.

To Increase Difficulty

• Move the target away from the side line.

Success Check

• Contact the right side of the ball.

• The racket head should point down when contacting the ball on the backhand serve and forehand serve.

• Watch the curved path of the ball to judge how much spin you are producing.

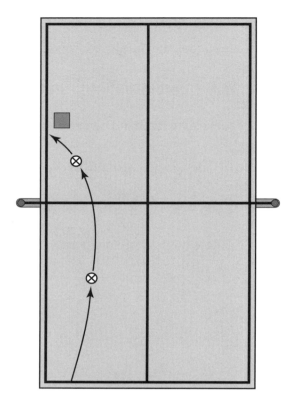

Score Your Success

17 to 20 successful forehand serves = 10 points

13 to 16 successful forehand serves = 5 points

9 to 12 successful forehand serves = 1 point

Your score ___

17 to 20 successful backhand serves = 10 points

13 to 16 successful backhand serves = 5 points

9 to 12 successful backhand serves = 1 point

Your score ___

Figure 5.15 Path of the ball during the mid-depth right sidespin serve drill.

Mid-Depth Serve Drill 3. *Mid-Depth Center Line Sidespin Serve*

For this drill, you will need two targets, one on the opponent's center line 1 foot (30 cm) from the end line, the other on the center line 18 inches (46 cm) closer to the net than the first target (figure 5.16). Using forehand sidespin serves, try to curve the serves between the two targets. Serve 10 right sidespin and 10 left sidespin serves.

To Increase Difficulty

• Move the targets closer together.

Success Check

• Watch the curved path of your serves to evaluate how much spin you produce.

• Try to start all forehand serves from the same position to make it difficult for your opponent to anticipate which serve is coming.

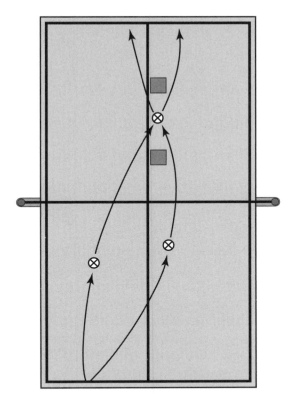

Figure 5.16 Path of the ball during the mid-depth center line sidespin serves drill.

DEEP SERVES

Deep serves must be placed deep into the corners on your opponent's side of the table or into the elbow of his playing arm to jam his return. Usually, deep serves are executed with the forehand serve motion.

When serving long, focus on producing good speed and placing the ball in the right location. On a deep serve, the first bounce on your side of the table should be close to your end line. To generate good speed, contact the ball with more force and less friction contact (figure 5.17). It should feel as though you are hitting through the ball.

When serving long, you will use your wrist less and your forearm more. Execute the forehand deep serve from your backhand corner. Use the forehand serve grip if you typically use a shake-hands grip. Players who use a pen-hold grip already have full use of the wrist, so no grip

Figure 5.17 Contact point for a forehand deep serve. The player hits through the center of the ball, producing speed and not much spin.

change is necessary. If your racket is slightly open at contact, you will produce a fast serve with back-spin. If your racket is slightly closed at contact, you will produce a fast serve with topspin.

Misstep

Your deep serve lacks speed.

Correction

Hit through the ball, using mostly your forearm.

To execute a forehand deep backspin serve (figure 5.18), take a position completely off to the left side of the table so that your left hand is located at the left side line. Use the serve grip. Place your left foot in front of your right (right-handed player). Your upper body should be parallel to the left side line. Your racket hand and free hand, which is holding the ball, are close together at the start of the serve.

From an open palm, toss the ball at least 6 inches (15 cm) high, and at the same time, rotate your upper body to the right, bringing the racket back into the backswing position. Immediately after the toss, remove your free hand from the area between your body and the table so that the ball is visible to your opponent throughout the serve.

As the ball begins to descend, rotate your body back to the left and bring the racket to the ball. Contact the ball at its center with a slightly open racket. Contact is primarily force, not friction, because you are trying to produce speed and only a slight amount of backspin. The arm swing is straight back and toward your target. The power for the deep serve comes from your forearm; not much wrist is used. The first bounce on your side of the table should be close to your end line. This will produce a deep serve on the opponent's side. After serving, quickly get into a ready position to take advantage of any loose return.

Figure 5.18   Forehand Deep Backspin Serve

BEGINNING POSITION

1. Stand outside left side line
2. Left foot in front of right foot
3. Upper body parallel to the left side line
4. Serve grip
5. Hands close together

a

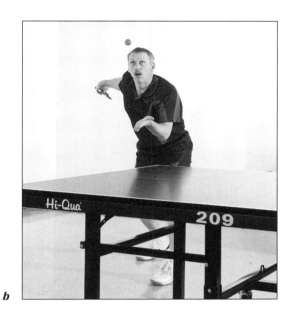

b

c

BACKSWING

1. Throw ball up
2. Rotate upper body to right
3. Remove free arm from space between body and table to allow opponent to see ball
4. Racket head points down
5. Racket head is slightly open
6. Transfer weight to back foot

CONTACT

1. Transfer weight to front foot
2. Rotate upper body to left, bringing racket to ball
3. Make contact at center of ball with slightly open racket, hitting through ball with force contact
4. Execute stroke with forearm and very little wrist

FOLLOW-THROUGH

1. Follow through straight toward target
2. Recover quickly to ready position

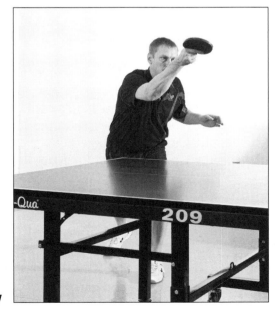

d

The forehand deep topspin serve is executed exactly as is the forehand deep backspin serve, except that the ball is contacted with a slightly closed racket (figure 5.19). The starting position, backswing, and follow-through are all the same as those of the forehand deep backspin serve.

Figure 5.19   Forehand Deep Topspin Serve

CONTACT

1. Transfer weight to front foot
2. Rotate upper body to left, bringing racket to ball
3. Remove free arm from area between body and table to allow receiver to see ball
4. Make contact at center of ball with slightly closed racket, hitting through ball with force contact
5. Execute stroke with forearm and little wrist

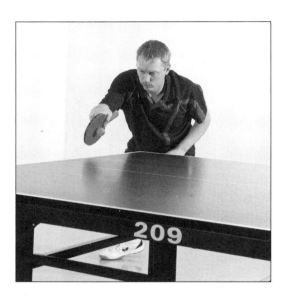

Deep Serve Drill 1. *Deep Serve*

Place a standard-size sheet of paper, as a target, on both the backhand and forehand corners of your opponent's side of the table (figure 5.20). Using the forehand deep serve technique, direct 20 fast backspin serves and 20 fast topspin serves toward the target in your opponent's backhand corner. Repeat, directing all serves to the target in your opponent's forehand corner. Keep track of how many times you hit the target.

To Increase Difficulty

- Decrease the size of the targets.

Success Check

- Make sure the bounce on your side of the table is close to your end line.
- Hit through the ball for maximum speed.

Score Your Success

17 to 20 successful forehand backspin serves to the backhand target = 10 points

13 to 16 successful forehand backspin serves to the backhand target = 5 points

9 to 12 successful forehand backspin serves to the backhand target = 1 point

Your score ___

17 to 20 successful forehand topspin serves to the backhand target = 10 points

13 to 16 successful forehand topspin serves to the backhand target = 5 points

9 to 12 successful forehand topspin serves to the backhand target = 1 point

Your score ___

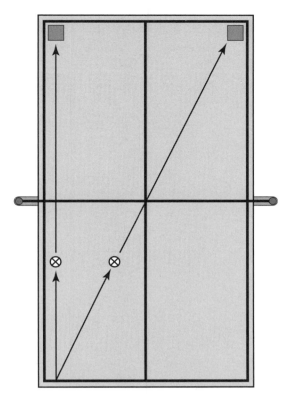

17 to 20 successful forehand backspin serves to the forehand target = 10 points

13 to 16 successful forehand backspin serves to the forehand target = 5 points

9 to 12 successful forehand backspin serves to the forehand target = 1 point

Your score ___

17 to 20 successful forehand topspin serves to the forehand target = 10 points

13 to 16 successful forehand topspin serves to the forehand target = 5 points

9 to 12 successful forehand topspin serves to the forehand target = 1 point

Your score ___

Figure 5.20 Target position and ball path for the deep serve drill.

Deep Serve Drill 2. *Mixed Short and Deep Serves*

For this drill, serve 20 balls, alternating between one short serve and one deep serve. You can direct the short serve anywhere on the table, but it should bounce at least three times before going off the table on the opponent's side. The deep serve should hit the target (a standard-size piece of paper) placed in the opponent's backhand corner (figure 5.21) and can have either backspin or topspin.

To Increase Difficulty

• Decrease the size of the target.

Success Check

• Try to execute both short and deep serves with as much of the same motion as possible.

• Try to not look where you are serving because it can tip off your opponent about where the ball is going.

• Focus on finding the correct first-bounce position on your side of the table.

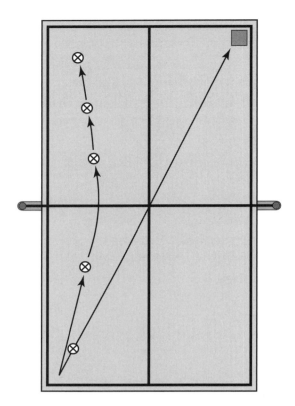

Figure 5.21   Mixed short and deep serves.

Deep Serve Drill 3. *Mixed Mid-Depth Sidespin and Deep Serves*

For this drill, you will need two targets (standard-size pieces of paper). Place one target in your opponent's backhand corner (figure 5.22). Place the second target midway between the first target and the center line on your opponent's backhand side line. Serve 20 forehand serves, alternating between a mid-depth left sidespin serve and a deep topspin serve. The sidespin serve should land on the table and curve to the left in front of the target before going off the side line. The deep serve should hit the target in the backhand corner.

To Increase Difficulty

- Decrease the size of the targets.

Success Check

- Try to execute both short and deep serves with as much of the same motion as possible.
- Try to not look where you are serving because it can tip off your opponent about where the ball is going.
- Focus on finding the correct first-bounce position on your side of the table.

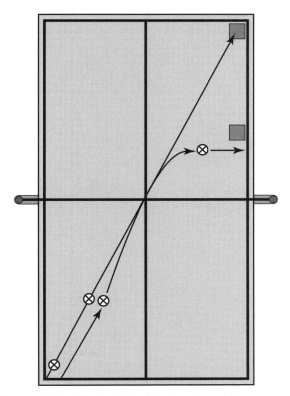

Figure 5.22 Mixed mid-depth sidespin and deep serves.

SUCCESS SUMMARY FOR SERVING

This step described the basic serves that all players need to execute: short serves, mid-depth serves, and deep serves. However, you will find that an almost endless number of serve variations and deliveries are possible. To become a good server, learn to enjoy experimenting with various serves and also to enjoy practicing serves. You don't even need a practice partner, just a bucket of balls and a table.

The serve drills featured in this step will help you learn to produce various spins on your serves and control the placement of your serves. To see whether you are ready to move on to step 6, add up your drill scores. If you scored at least 120 points, you are ready to move on to step 6. If not, you need more practice.

Short Serve Drills

1. Short Backspin Serve	___ out of 20
2. Ball Placement	___ out of 20

Mid-Depth Serve Drills

1. Mid-Depth Left Sidespin Serve	___ out of 20
2. Mid-Depth Right Sidespin Serve	___ out of 20
3. Mid-Depth Center Line Sidespin Serve	___ out of 10

Deep Serve Drills

1. Deep Serve	___ out of 40
2. Mixed Short and Deep Serves	___ out of 10
3. Mixed Mid-Depth Sidespin and Deep Serves	___ out of 10
Total	**___ out of 150**

All points in a game begin with either serving or returning the serve. This makes the serve and serve return the two most important strokes in the game. This step covered the basics of becoming a good server. The next step focuses on how to effectively return your opponent's serves. If you master these two steps, you will be on your way to becoming a high-level player.

Returning Serve

When receiving an opponent's serve, your goal is to return the ball in such a way that you stop his attack and take control of the point. Because 50 percent of all points start with you receiving serve, this is a critical part of the game to master.

Producing effective serve returns requires several skills, including the following:

- Being in the correct serve receive position
- Reading the type and amount of spin the server puts on the ball
- Returning sidespin serves effectively
- Returning the serve to the correct target
- Performing the drop and flip strokes

GETTING IN SERVE RETURN POSITION

The server's position when serving dictates where you should stand to receive the serve. If your opponent is serving from his backhand corner, shift your ready position so you can cover wide-angle serves to your backhand (figure 6.1a). If the server is serving more from the middle of the table, shift your ready position so that your racket arm is at the center of the table (figure 6.1b). If the server is left-handed or is serving from the left side of the table, shift your ready position so that your playing arm is several inches (or centimeters) to the right of the center line of the table (figure 6.1c).

Wherever you stand to receive serve, make sure you are not too close to the table to return a deep, fast serve. Moving forward to return a short serve is much easier than moving back to return a fast, long serve. For this reason, always set up at least an arm's length away from the table (figure 6.2). This is far enough back so you can easily return any deep serve. If the ball is short, you can easily step in to make the return.

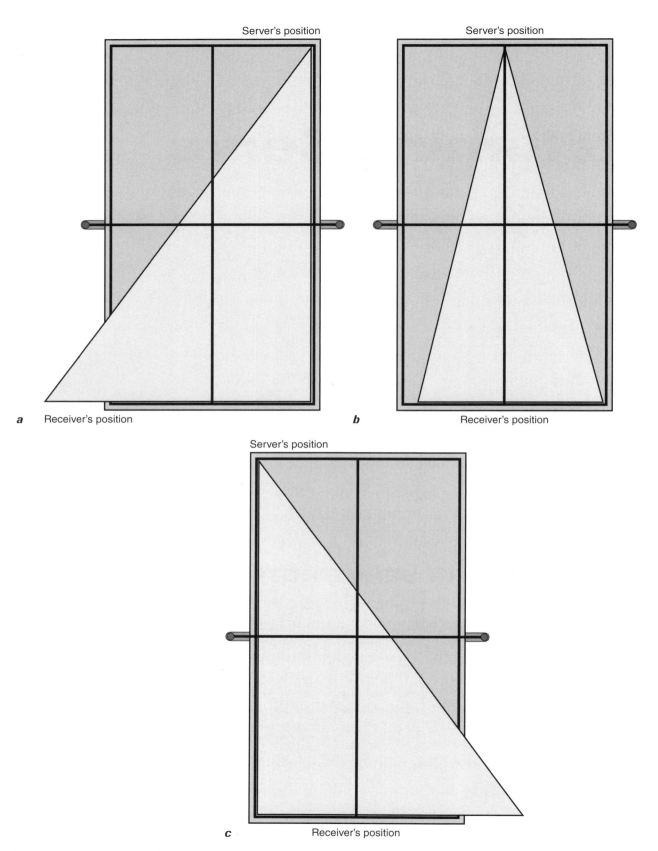

Figure 6.1 Serve angles when the server is *(a)* standing in his backhand corner; *(b)* standing in the middle of the table; *(c)* left-handed or serving from the left side of the table.

Figure 6.2 Correct distance from the table in serve return position.

READING THE SPIN ON THE SERVE

In step 5, you learned how to perform the basic serves of the game by contacting various parts of the ball with the racket. This understanding of how the various spins are produced is critical to effectively returning serves. To be able to judge the type and amount of the spin on your opponent's serve, you must do the following:

- Watch the racket angle at contact. If the racket angle is closed, then the serve will have topspin. If it is open, the serve will have backspin.

- Watch where the racket contacts the ball. If the racket contacts the ball on the left or right side, then sidespin will occur. Normally, sidespin is combined with either backspin or topspin.

- Watch the amount of racket acceleration on contact with the ball. The greater the racket acceleration is, the more spin there will be on the ball. This acceleration comes from a snapping action of the wrist, so pay attention to how much your opponent uses her wrist.

- Watch the label on the ball. If you can see the label on the ball, little or no spin is on the serve. If you cannot see the label, the serve has a lot of spin.

- Watch the path of the ball between the first and second bounce. The path the ball takes between the first and second bounces can help you judge the spin on the ball. If the ball curves right or left, the serve has sidespin. If the ball stays low between the two bounces, the serve has some topspin. If the ball rises somewhat between the two bounces, the serve has some backspin.

RETURNING SIDESPIN SERVES

For developing players, sidespin serves are the most difficult to return effectively. Deep topspin or backspin serves can be returned using the basic strokes you learned in step 4. However, when sidespin is added to any serve, you must adjust your racket angle to counteract the spin. This is true no matter which serve return stroke you choose to use. This skill takes a lot of practice to learn.

The easiest way to return a sidespin serve is to stop your opponent's spin by contacting the correct side of the ball. As discussed in step 4, to return your opponent's right sidespin, angle your racket to contact the left side of the ball (figure 6.3a) and then execute the return stroke you wish to use. Note that you are contacting the same side of the ball as your opponent did to produce the spin. To return your opponent's left sidespin, angle your racket to contact the right side of the ball (figure 6.3b). Note that, again, you are contacting the same side of the ball as your opponent did to produce the spin. In other words, you are trying to be like a mirror image of your opponent, contacting the ball on the same location that he did, thus stopping the sidespin on the ball. If you have contacted the correct location on the ball, you will stop your opponent's sidespin. When this happens, your return will travel in a straight line and the ball will feel light on your racket. If you touch the wrong side of the ball, the ball will jump sideways off your racket and feel heavy.

Figure 6.3   Sidespin Serve Return

a

b

RIGHT SIDESPIN SERVE

1. Contact ball (represented by wheel) on right side to produce right sidespin serve
2. Receiver touches ball (wheel) on same side to stop sidespin

LEFT SIDESPIN SERVE

1. Contact ball (represented by wheel) on left side to produce left sidespin serve
2. Receiver touches ball (wheel) on same side to stop sidespin

Backhand Serve Return Drill 1. *Returning Backhand Deep Left Sidespin Serves*

From his backhand corner, your training partner serves deep backspin serves with left sidespin deep into your backhand corner. Your goal is to touch the bottom right side of the ball to stop his spin and return the ball in a straight line to his backhand corner. To contact the right side of the ball, you must bend your wrist back toward your body. First use the backhand push stroke on the return; then use the backhand topspin stroke. Complete 20 returns total.

To Increase Difficulty

• Ask your practice partner to increase the amount of spin on the serves.

To Decrease Difficulty

• Ask your practice partner to decrease the amount of spin on the serves.

Success Check

• Contact the bottom right side of the ball. If you do this properly, the ball should return in a straight line.
• Use the correct backhand push or backhand topspin stroke to return the serve.

Score Your Success

9 or 10 successful backhand push stroke returns = 10 points

7 or 8 successful backhand push stroke returns = 5 points

5 or 6 successful backhand push stroke returns = 1 point

9 or 10 successful backhand topspin stroke returns = 10 points

7 or 8 successful backhand topspin stroke returns = 5 points

5 or 6 successful backhand topspin stroke returns = 1 point

Your score ___

Backhand Serve Return Drill 2. *Returning Deep Right Sidespin Serves*

Have your training partner serve 20 deep serves with right sidespin to your backhand. She can use either forehand or backhand serves. Your goal is to touch the bottom left side of the ball to stop the spin and return the serve straight to her backhand. Return the first 10 serves with a backhand push. For the second 10, use a backhand topspin return.

To Increase Difficulty

• Ask your practice partner to increase the amount of spin on the serves.

To Decrease Difficulty

• Ask your practice partner to decrease the amount of spin on the serves.

Success Check

• Contact the bottom left side of the ball. If you do this properly, the ball should return in a straight line.
• Use the correct backhand push or backhand topspin stroke to return the serve.

Score Your Success

9 or 10 successful backhand push stroke returns = 10 points

7 or 8 successful backhand push stroke returns = 5 points

5 or 6 successful backhand push stroke returns = 1 point

9 or 10 successful backhand topspin stroke returns = 10 points

7 or 8 successful backhand topspin stroke returns = 5 points

5 or 6 successful backhand topspin stroke returns = 1 point

Your score ___

Forehand Serve Return Drill 1. *Returning Forehand Deep Left Sidespin Serves*

From his backhand corner, your training partner serves deep backspin serves with left sidespin into your forehand corner. Your goal is to touch the bottom right side of the ball to stop his spin and return the ball in a straight line to his backhand corner. For the first 10 returns, use the forehand push stroke. For the next 10, use the forehand topspin stroke. Complete 20 returns total.

To Increase Difficulty

- Ask your practice partner to increase the amount of spin on the serves.

To Decrease Difficulty

- Ask your practice partner to decrease the amount of spin on the serves.

Success Check

- Contact the bottom right side of the ball. If you do this properly, the ball should return in a straight line.
- Use the correct forehand push or forehand topspin stroke to return the serve.

Score Your Success

9 or 10 successful forehand push stroke returns = 10 points

7 or 8 successful forehand push stroke returns = 5 points

5 or 6 successful forehand push stroke returns = 1 point

9 or 10 successful forehand topspin stroke returns = 10 points

7 or 8 successful forehand topspin stroke returns = 5 points

5 or 6 successful forehand topspin stroke returns = 1 point

Your score ___

Forehand Serve Return Drill 2. *Returning Forehand Deep Right Sidespin Serves*

From his backhand corner, your training partner serves deep backspin serves with right sidespin into your forehand corner. Your goal is to touch the bottom left side of the ball to stop his spin and return the ball in a straight line to his backhand corner. To touch this location, you will need to bend your wrist back toward your right. For the first 10 returns, use the forehand push stroke. For the next 10, use the forehand topspin stroke. Complete 20 returns total.

To Increase Difficulty

- Ask your practice partner to increase the amount of spin on the serves.

To Decrease Difficulty

- Ask your practice partner to decrease the amount of spin on the serves.

Success Check

- Contact the bottom left side of the ball. If you do this properly, the ball should return in a straight line.
- Use the correct forehand push or forehand topspin stroke to return the serve.

Score Your Success

9 or 10 successful forehand push stroke returns = 10 points

7 or 8 successful forehand push stroke returns = 5 points

5 or 6 successful forehand push stroke returns = 1 point

9 or 10 successful forehand topspin stroke returns = 10 points

7 or 8 successful forehand topspin stroke returns = 5 points

5 or 6 successful forehand topspin stroke returns = 1 point

Your score ___

RETURNING TO THE BEST LOCATION

When returning any serve, be very careful about the location of the return. When hitting a deep return, get the ball into the corner, or better yet, have it break the side line between the net and the corner (figure 6.4). This is called "cutting the corner." If your opponent is not quick on his feet, a fast return into the playing elbow will be effective. By cutting the corners with your returns, you can also anticipate that your opponent's returns will go crosscourt and you can move early into position to attack them.

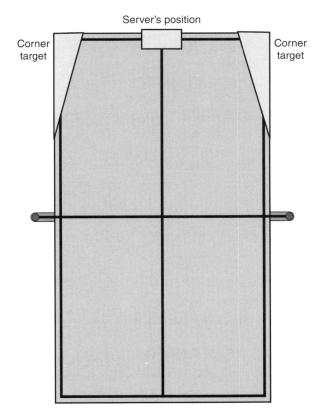

Figure 6.4 Deep target areas for backhand and forehand serve returns.

EXECUTING THE DROP RETURN

Making a short return off an opponent's short serve, also called a drop shot, often is the key to being able to control and win a point. This stroke looks deceptively simple, but in reality, it takes a lot of skill and practice to master.

When returning a short serve return to your opponent, the key is to keep the ball very short, making it difficult for your opponent to attack. An effective short return, or drop return, also stays low after bouncing.

Three Basic Elements for the Drop Return

How to touch the ball = at first, touch the ball as if you were trying to just stop it; as your hand skills develop, add some of your own spin by making friction contact with the ball

When to touch the ball = as it is rising

Where to touch the ball = against a short backspin serve, use a slightly downward motion to touch the ball at its center as it is on the rise; against a short backspin sidespin serve, touch near the center of the ball but move your contact point toward the side where the spin is coming from and use a downward and slightly sideways stroke to stop your opponent's spin

Misstep

You are unable to make a short return to your opponent.

Correction

Make sure you contact the ball early while it is on the rise.

Right-handed players execute most drop returns, both backhand and forehand, by stepping in with the right foot. The exception to this would be when your opponent's ball is short and wide to your backhand. In this case, step in with the left leg down the side of the table.

The drop return (figures 6.5 and 6.6) begins from the ready position. As you recognize that your opponent's serve will be short, step under the table with the right foot (right-handed player), getting as close to the ball as possible. Your attacker's ready position will put you in position to cover about two-thirds of the table with

the forehand, which holds true when returning short serves as well. Keeping your elbow bent, contact the ball immediately off the bounce with an open racket and make a slight downward motion with your wrist. Be sure to get close to the ball. Do not extend your forearm to reach for the ball. The farther away you are from the ball, the more difficult it will be to control your return. The goal is to drop the ball short and low back to your opponent, making it difficult for him to attack. A good drop return can force an opponent to return the next ball deeper, allowing you to attack first.

Figure 6.5 | Backhand Drop Return

SERVE RETURN POSITION

1. Recognize short serve to backhand
2. Prepare to step under table to move close to ball
3. Bend racket arm and bring head close to racket
4. Hold racket a little higher than ball
5. Racket face is slightly open

a

b

c

CONTACT

1. Contact ball while it is rising
2. Racket contacts ball around center of ball's face

STROKE AND RECOVERY

1. Stroke is very short
2. Racket travels downward, not under ball
3. Weight on front foot
4. Push off front foot to recover to ready position
5. Recover to ready position before opponent touches ball

Misstep

The ball jumps sideways on contact with the racket.

Correction

Adjust your racket angle to stop the sidespin on the ball.

Figure 6.6   Forehand Drop Return

SERVE RETURN POSITION

1. Recognize short serve to forehand
2. Prepare to step under table to move close to ball
3. Bend racket arm and bring head close to racket
4. Racket is a little higher than ball
5. Racket face is slightly open

a

(continued)

Figure 6.6   *(continued)*

b

c

CONTACT

1. Contact ball while it is rising
2. Racket contacts ball around center of ball's face

STROKE AND RECOVERY

1. Stroke is short
2. Racket travels downward, not under ball
3. Weight on front foot
4. Push off with front foot to recover to ready position
5. Recover to ready position before opponent touches ball

Misstep

After the stroke, you have trouble recovering quickly to the ready position.

Correction

When making contact with the ball, make sure your weight is on your right foot. Push back hard off that foot to return to the ready position.

The next three drills will help you master the correct stroke and footwork needed to execute a quality short drop return.

Drop Return Drill 1. *Touch the Line*

This drill helps teach the concept of taking the ball early. It also helps to develop good footwork and the rhythm for the drop shot. Use only half the table. You and your drill partner stand at the sides of the table in the ready position. Using proper footwork, one player steps in and touches the center line with his racket. He immediately returns to the ready position the correct distance from the table. As soon as he touches the line, the other player begins to move forward and touches the line. Continue to alternate, touching the line and recovering. The recovery is very important because you do not want to be caught over the table if your opponent attacks your return. Recover to the ready position before your partner touches the center line. Practice for 3 minutes.

To Increase Difficulty

- Have your practice partner speed up his movements.

To Decrease Difficulty

- Have your practice partner slow down his movements.

Success Check

- Do not move forward until your partner touches the white line.
- Push off with your front foot when you return to the ready position.

Score Your Success

Execute the drill for 3 minutes. Ask your practice partner to evaluate your form and movement and rate your performance on a scale from 1 (lowest) to 10 (highest).

Earn 8 to 10 rating = 10 points

Earn 5 to 7 rating = 5 points

Earn 1 to 4 rating = 1 point

Your score ___

Drop Return Drill 2. *Touch the Ball*

Perform this drill the same as touch the line, but this time place a ball on the center line. Each player steps in and tries to just barely touch the ball with his racket (figure 6.7). Try to keep the ball as close to the center line as possible. This drill helps develop a light touch and ball control, which are necessary for playing drop shots. Practice for 3 minutes.

Figure 6.7 Touch the ball drill.

To Increase Difficulty

- Have your practice partner speed up his movements.

To Decrease Difficulty

- Have your practice partner slow down his movements.

Success Check

- Do not move forward until your partner touches the white line.
- Push off with your front foot when you return to the ready position.
- Check to see that you are using a light touch on the ball so it stays close to the white line.

Score Your Success

Execute the drill for 3 minutes. Ask your practice partner to evaluate your form and movement and rate your performance on a scale from 1 (lowest) to 10 (highest).

Earn 8 to 10 rating = 10 points

Earn 5 to 7 rating = 5 points

Earn 1 to 4 rating = 1 point

Your score ___

Drop Return Drill 3. *Serve and Drop*

Have your practice partner serve 10 short back-spin serves to your backhand and 10 to your forehand. Your goal is execute a drop return so that the ball, if left untouched, would bounce at least three times on your opponent's side of the table before passing the end line. Your return should stay low after the bounce. You can direct the return anywhere on the table as long as the return is short.

To Increase Difficulty

- Have your practice partner add some side-spin to the serves.

Success Check

- Step in and get close to the ball.
- Contact the center of the ball while it is on the rise.
- Make sure your returns are low and short.

Score Your Success

9 or 10 successful backhand drop returns = 10 points

7 or 8 successful backhand drop returns = 5 points

5 or 6 successful backhand drop returns = 1 point

9 or 10 successful forehand drop returns = 10 points

7 or 8 successful forehand drop returns = 5 points

5 or 6 successful forehand drop returns = 1 point

Your score ___

EXECUTING THE FLIP RETURN

In today's game, the ability to attack a short serve is becoming more important. The flip return is a short topspin stroke played mostly with the wrist and forearm. Because the body is blocked by the table, the lower body cannot be used to generate power for this stroke. For this reason, the success of the flip return relies on hitting the targets shown in figure 6.4 (page 103). These targets are the deep corners or into the opponent's racket arm at the elbow.

Three Basic Elements for the Flip Return

How to touch the ball = make friction (spin) contact with the ball, producing a light top-spin; at contact, your forearm should be moving upward and forward

When to touch the ball = at the top of the bounce

Where to touch the ball = against a short backspin serve, contact the ball below its center; against a short backspin serve with sidespin, contact the ball below its center but move your contact point toward the side where the sidespin is coming from; against a no-spin serve, contact the center of the ball; against a short topspin serve, contact above the center of the ball

Execute the stroke using mostly the forearm and some wrist. Most of the force comes from snapping the forearm, which should be moving upward at the moment of contact. The racket face should be somewhat open against a back-spin serve and neutral against a no-spin serve.

The flip return (figures 6.8 and 6.9) begins from the ready position. As you recognize that the serve will be short, either to your backhand or forehand, begin stepping toward the ball. For most short serves, except those to the wide backhand, step in with the right foot. Work to get your right foot under the table close to the spot where the ball contacts the table. For serves wide to your forehand, you may need to use side steps first and then step in to get close to the ball. To be effective, approach the backhand

and forehand flip returns in the same manner you would if you were going to make a drop return. Bend your racket elbow and hold the racket open slightly. At the last moment, when the ball reaches the top of the bounce, snap your forearm and wrist upward to flip the ball back deep into the opponent's corner or directly into the elbow of his racket arm.

When executing a forehand flip, rotate your upper body to the right so that your left shoulder is closer to the net (closed position). Approaching the ball in this position allows you to direct the return to all areas of the table with power. If you approach with your shoulders open you will only be able to place the ball crosscourt with power and your opponent will know where your returns are going. Remember to recover back to the ready position; this is an essential part of the stroke. You do not want to get caught leaning over the table when your opponent returns the ball.

Figure 6.8   Forehand Flip Return

SERVE RETURN POSITION

1. Recognize short serve to forehand
2. Step forward to get close to ball
3. Rotate shoulders to closed position
4. Bend racket arm and hold racket slightly open
5. Head is close to ball
6. Server can't tell if receiver will make a drop return or a flip

a

CONTACT

1. Contact ball at top of bounce
2. Racket moves upward when it contacts ball
3. Racket makes friction contact with ball
4. Rotate shoulders back to left to help provide power to stroke

b

STROKE AND RECOVERY

1. Produce stroke primarily with forearm and wrist
2. Stroke continues toward target
3. Push off front foot to recover to ready position
4. Return to ready position before opponent contacts ball

c

Misstep

Your flip return goes into the net.

Correction

Make sure to contact the ball at the top of the bounce.

Figure 6.9   Backhand Flip Return

SERVE RETURN POSITION

1. Recognize short serve to backhand
2. Step forward to get close to ball
3. Rotate shoulders to open position
4. Bend racket arm and hold racket slightly open
5. Head is close to ball
6. Server can't tell if receiver will make drop return or flip

a

CONTACT

1. Contact ball at top of bounce
2. Racket moves upward when it contacts ball
3. Racket makes friction contact with ball

b

STROKE AND RECOVERY

1. Produce stroke primarily with forearm and wrist
2. Stroke continues toward target
3. Push off front foot to recover to ready position
4. Return to ready position before opponent contacts ball

c

Misstep

Your flip return goes long, missing the table.

Correction

Make sure your racket and forearm are moving upward when you contact the ball to produce topspin on your return.

Flip Return Drill 1. *Forehand Flip Returns Crosscourt*

Have your practice partner serve 10 short backspin serves to your forehand. As your skill progresses, ask her to add some sidespin to the serves. Return the serves crosscourt using a forehand flip return, cutting the angle between the net and the end line of the table.

To Increase Difficulty

- Have your practice partner add some sidespin to the serves.

Success Check

- Get close to the ball by stepping in.
- Contact the ball at the top of the bounce with your racket moving upward.

- Make sure your shoulders are in a closed position when you contact the ball.
- Follow through toward your target.
- Recover to the ready position after each return.

Score Your Success

9 or 10 successful crosscourt forehand flip returns = 10 points

7 or 8 successful crosscourt forehand flip returns = 5 points

5 or 6 successful crosscourt forehand flip returns = 1 point

Your score ___

Flip Return Drill 2. *Forehand Flip Returns Down the Line*

Place a standard size piece of paper into the opponent's backhand corner as a target. Have your practice partner serve 10 short backspin serves to your forehand. As your skill progresses, ask him to add some sidespin to the serves. Return the serves down the line to the target using forehand flip returns.

To Increase Difficulty

- Have your practice partner add some sidespin to the serves.

Success Check

- Get close to the ball by stepping in.
- Contact the ball at the top of the bounce with your racket moving upward.

- Make sure your shoulders are in a closed position when you contact the ball.
- Follow through toward your target.
- Recover to the ready position after each return.

Score Your Success

9 or 10 successful down-the-line forehand flip returns = 10 points

7 or 8 successful down-the-line forehand flip returns = 5 points

5 or 6 successful down-the-line forehand flip returns = 1 point

Your score ___

Flip Return Drill 3. *Backhand Flip Returns Crosscourt*

Ask your practice partner to send 10 short backspin serves to your backhand side. Using a backhand flip, return the ball so it breaks the side line between the net and the end line of the table.

To Increase Difficulty

- Have your practice partner add some sidespin to the serves.

Success Check

- Get close to the ball by stepping in.
- Contact the ball at the top of the bounce with your racket moving upward.
- Make sure your shoulders are in an open position when you contact the ball.

- Follow through toward your target.
- Recover to the ready position after each return.

Score Your Success

9 or 10 successful crosscourt backhand flip returns = 10 points

7 or 8 successful crosscourt backhand flip returns = 5 points

5 or 6 successful crosscourt backhand flip returns = 1 point

Your score ___

Flip Return Drill 4. *Backhand Flip Returns Down the Line*

Place a standard-size piece of paper into the opponent's forehand corner as a target. Ask your practice partner to send 10 short backspin serves to your backhand side. Direct your returns to the paper target using a backhand flip.

To Increase Difficulty

- Have your practice partner add some sidespin to her serves.

Success Check

- Get close to the ball by stepping in.
- Contact the ball at the top of the bounce with your racket moving upward.

- Make sure your shoulders are in an open position when you contact the ball.
- Follow through toward your target.
- Recover to the ready position after each return.

Score Your Success

9 or 10 successful down-the-line backhand flip returns = 10 points

7 or 8 successful down-the-line backhand flip returns = 5 points

5 or 6 successful down-the-line backhand flip returns = 1 point

Your score ___

SUCCESS SUMMARY OF RETURNING SERVE

Every point in table tennis starts when you either serve or return serve. A strong serve return can take your opponent out of his normal game and put him on the defensive. Although serve returns are not the most fun strokes to practice, working on returns is a quick way to improve your success in match play.

The drills in this step will help you develop basic serve return strokes and understand the concepts. To see whether you are ready to move on to step 7, add up your drill scores. If you scored at least 130 points, you are ready to move on to step 7. If not, practice more until you score at least 130 points.

Backhand Serve Return Drills

1. Returning Backhand Deep Left Sidespin Serves	___ out of 20
2. Returning Deep Right Sidespin Serves	___ out of 20

Forehand Serve Return Drills

1. Returning Forehand Deep Left Sidespin Serves	___ out of 20
2. Returning Forehand Deep Right Sidespin Serves	___ out of 20

Drop Return Drills

1. Touch the Line	___ out of 10
2. Touch the Ball	___ out of 10
3. Serve and Drop	___ out of 20

Flip Return Drills

1. Forehand Flip Returns Crosscourt	___ out of 10
2. Forehand Flip Returns Down the Line	___ out of 10
3. Backhand Flip Returns Crosscourt	___ out of 10
4. Backhand Flip Returns Down the Line	___ out of 10
Total	___ *out of 160*

By this point, you have learned the basic strokes, serves, and serve returns. Your challenge now is to combine all of these skills to actually start playing games. Step 7 introduces a unique training method that will teach you how to link these strokes to play and win points.

Using the Five-Ball Training System

In previous steps, you learned the basic strokes of the game, including serves and serve returns, as well as how to move. In this step, all you have learned will be combined as you learn how to play and win actual points.

Although it is important to practice each stroke individually to learn the technique and establish ball control, all points are played in a set sequence of strokes. For example, you start every point by either serving or returning the serve. You may have a strong forehand topspin, but you must combine it with a good serve or serve return to be effective.

Research has shown that 80 percent of all points in table tennis end by the fifth stroke. Even if the point continues past the fifth stroke, one player usually is in a winning position at the fifth stroke. The goal of this step is to move you from executing one stroke at a time to planning out whole points. Until now, drills have been relatively simple, focusing on one stroke at a time. As you gain control of your strokes, you should practice them in the sequence in which they will occur during a point. These sequences, or patterns, can be developed by using the five-ball training system. This is the most common form of practice used by intermediate and advanced players.

To understand how this five-stroke pattern works, let's take a closer look at how the first five balls of every point can form patterns of play.

First Five Strokes of Every Point

First ball: Serve

Second ball: Serve return

Third ball: First attack for server

Fourth ball: First defensive stroke or counter-attack for receiver

Fifth ball: Second attack for server

As you can see, the server controls the first, third, and fifth balls. The receiver controls the second and fourth balls. Both the server and the receiver try to use each touch of the ball to set up their next stroke. Both have the goal to get their strongest strokes into the game to win the point as soon as possible. To practice and learn these patterns of play, my students use a method I call the five-ball training system.

UNDERSTANDING THE FIVE-BALL TRAINING SYSTEM

For this type of practice, two players work together. One player, the attacker, does each drill. The other player, the feeder, feeds balls to the attacker in a set pattern. Each drill focuses on one of the first five strokes listed earlier. All strokes leading up to the one being focused on are predetermined so that the ball goes to the same location every time. After executing the featured stroke, the attacker tries to win the point and can play that stroke anywhere on the table. If the feeder can return the ball, the two play out the point. The same pattern is repeated, usually for five to seven minutes of practice. At this time, the two players switch roles and the feeder becomes the attacker.

The goal of this type of practice is to link strokes so that they happen automatically during a point. This allows players to create their own favorite patterns of play based on their strongest shots. The patterns you learn eventually will become the basis for the development of your own style of play.

Many possible patterns can be created within the first five strokes of each point, far too many to list. However, a few patterns that occur often for most players should be part of everyone's practice. As you gain experience with this type of practice, you will develop your own personal favorites.

Misstep

The attacker is able to complete less than 75 percent of the strokes in the drill.

Correction

The feeder needs to provide easier returns with less speed or spin.

Misstep

The attacker wins less than 50 percent of the points.

Correction

The attacker should focus on the placement of the main stroke. The target areas are the deep corners, cutting the side line of the table when possible, and deep into the opponent's playing elbow.

Fifth-Ball Drill 1. *Fifth Ball With Two Forehand Topspins*

This drill also provides important practice switching between attacking a backspin return and then attacking a topspin return. This pattern is one of the most common that occurs in the game. Perform the pattern 10 times; then reverse roles.

- First ball: The attacker sends a short backspin serve to the feeder's backhand (figure 7.1).
- Second ball: The feeder pushes long to the attacker's backhand.
- Third ball: The attacker steps around and uses his forehand to produce a slow, heavy topspin to the feeder's backhand.

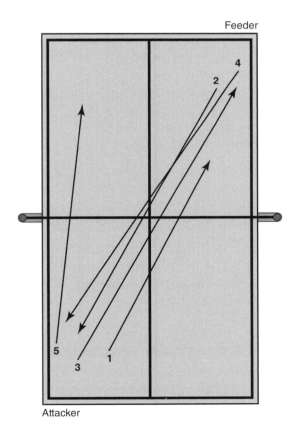

Figure 7.1 Ball placement during the fifth ball with two forehand topspins drill.

- Fourth ball: The feeder uses a backhand counter to return the ball to the attacker's backhand side.
- Fifth ball: The attacker makes a fast forehand topspin and tries to win the point. This stroke can be placed anywhere on the feeder's side of the table. If the ball is returned, the two play out the point.

To Increase Difficulty

- Have the feeder increase the amount of spin on the push.
- Have the feeder increase the speed of the backhand counter return.

To Decrease Difficulty

- Have the feeder reduce the amount of spin on the push.
- Have the feeder decrease the speed of the backhand counter return.

Success Check

- The first forehand topspin should have maximum spin. Contact the ball as it descends.
- The second forehand topspin should have maximum speed. Contact the ball at the top of the bounce.
- Use the proper pivot footwork.

Score Your Success

Note how many times out of 10 tries you successfully executed all of the strokes in the pattern. Do not count misses by the feeder.

9 or 10 successful patterns = 10 points

7 or 8 successful patterns = 5 points

5 or 6 successful patterns = 1 point

Your score ___

Fifth-Ball Drill 2. *Fifth Ball With Two Backhand Topspins*

Perform the pattern 10 times; then reverse roles. This drill follows the same pattern as the first drill except that the attacker uses backhand topspins instead of forehand topspins. Again, this drill provides practice combining an opening attack against a backspin return and then attacking the resulting topspin return.

- First ball: The attacker sends a short backspin serve to the feeder's backhand (figure 7.2).
- Second ball: The feeder pushes a long return to the attacker's backhand.
- Third ball: The attacker makes a slow, controlled backhand topspin return to the feeder's backhand side.

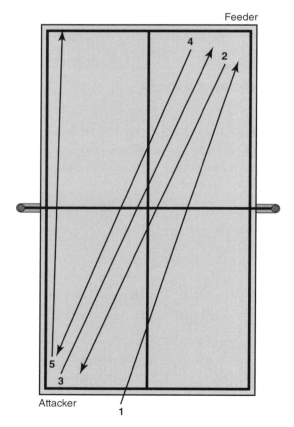

Figure 7.2 Ball placement during the fifth ball with two backhand topspins drill.

- Fourth ball: The feeder returns the ball crosscourt using a backhand counter to the attacker's backhand side.
- Fifth ball: The attacker makes a fast backhand topspin or fast counterdrive to try to win the point. This stroke can be placed anywhere on the feeder's side of the table. If the ball is returned, the two play out the point.

To Increase Difficulty

- Have the feeder increase the amount of spin on the push.
- Have the feeder increase the speed of the backhand counter return.

To Decrease Difficulty

- Have the feeder decrease the amount of spin on the push.
- Have the feeder decrease the speed of the backhand counter return.

Success Check

- Use your legs to provide the lift when you execute a backhand topspin against backspin.
- Contact the first backhand topspin as the ball descends to produce maximum topspin.
- Contact the second backhand topspin at the top of the bounce to generate maximum speed.

Score Your Success

Note how many times out of 10 tries you successfully executed all of the strokes in the pattern. Do not count misses by the feeder.

9 or 10 successful patterns = 10 points

7 or 8 successful patterns = 5 points

5 or 6 successful patterns = 1 point

Your score ____

Fifth-Ball Drill 3. *Fifth Ball With One Backhand Topspin and One Forehand Topspin*

In this drill, you practice combining an opening backhand topspin to force a weak return and then finishing the point with a strong forehand topspin. Perform the pattern 10 times; then reverse roles.

- First ball: The attacker sends a mid-depth backspin serve to the feeder's backhand (figure 7.3).
- Second ball: The feeder returns crosscourt using a backhand flip return.

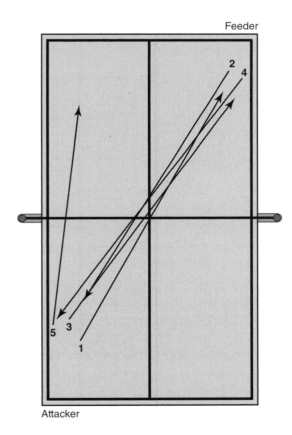

Attacker

Figure 7.3 Ball placement during the fifth ball with one backhand topspin and one forehand topspin drill.

- Third ball: The attacker returns crosscourt using a backhand topspin.
- Fourth ball: The feeder returns crosscourt using a backhand counterdrive.
- Fifth ball: The attacker steps around the table and makes a fast forehand topspin return to try to win the point. This return can be placed anywhere. If the ball is returned, the two play out the point.

To Increase Difficulty

- Have the feeder increase the speed of the backhand counterdrive return.

To Decrease Difficulty

- Have the feeder decrease the speed of the backhand counterdrive return.

Success Check

- Your backhand topspin return should cross the side line of the table between the feeder's backhand and the net.
- When executing the forehand topspin, contact the ball at the top of the bounce to produce full power on your return.

Score Your Success

Note how many times out of 10 tries you successfully executed all of the strokes in the pattern. Do not count misses by the feeder.

9 or 10 successful patterns = 10 points

7 or 8 successful patterns = 5 points

5 or 6 successful patterns = 1 point

Your score ____

Fifth-Ball Drill 4. *Fifth Ball With Backhand Counterdrive and Forehand Topspin*

This drill combines a deep serve and a fast backhand counterdrive with a finishing forehand topspin, all executed from your backhand corner. Perform the pattern 10 times; then reverse roles.

- First ball: The attacker sends a long, fast topspin–sidespin serve to the feeder's backhand (figure 7.4).
- Second ball: The feeder returns crosscourt using a backhand topspin.
- Third ball: The attacker returns crosscourt using a backhand counterdrive.

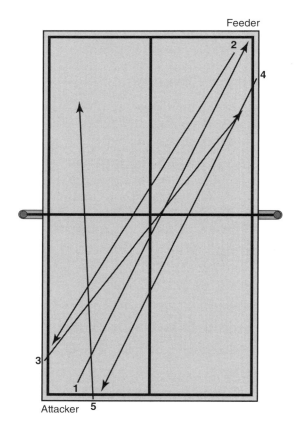

Figure 7.4 Ball placement during the fifth ball with backhand counterdrive and forehand topspin drill.

- Fourth ball: The feeder returns crosscourt using a backhand counterdrive.
- Fifth ball: The attacker steps around the table and plays a strong forehand topspin to anywhere on the feeder's side to try to win the point. If the ball is returned, the two play out the point.

To Increase Difficulty

- Have the feeder increase the amount of spin on the backhand returns.
- Have the feeder increase the speed of the backhand returns.

To Decrease Difficulty

- Have the feeder decrease the amount of spin on the backhand returns.
- Have the feeder decrease the speed of the backhand returns.

Success Check

- Hit your backhand counterdrive firmly at second-gear speed.
- Your backhand counterdrive return should cross the side line of the table between the feeder's backhand and the net.
- When executing the forehand topspin, contact the ball at the top of the bounce to produce full power on your return.

Score Your Success

Note how many times out of 10 tries you successfully executed all of the strokes in the pattern. Do not count misses by the feeder.

9 or 10 successful patterns = 10 points

7 or 8 successful patterns = 5 points

5 or 6 successful patterns = 1 point

Your score ____

120

Fifth-Ball Drill 5. *Fifth Ball With Forehand Flip Return and Forehand Countertopspin*

In this drill, the attacker flips the serve return out wide to the feeder's forehand; then anticipates a return crosscourt, trying to finish the point with a forehand countertopspin. Perform the pattern 10 times; then reverse roles.

- First ball: The attacker gives a short backspin serve to the feeder's forehand (figure 7.5).
- Second ball: The feeder returns crosscourt with a short drop return.

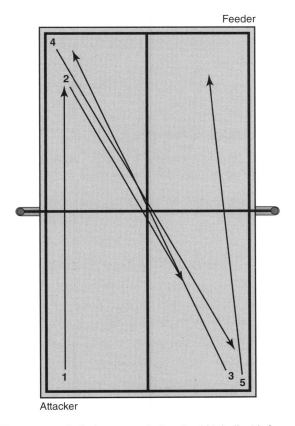

Figure 7.5 Ball placement during the fifth ball with forehand flip return and forehand countertopspin drill.

- Third ball: The attacker hits a deep return crosscourt using a forehand flip return.
- Fourth ball: The feeder returns crosscourt using a forehand topspin.
- Fifth ball: The attacker plays a strong forehand countertopspin return to anywhere on the feeder's side to try to win the point. If the ball is returned, the two play out the point.

To Increase Difficulty

- Have the feeder vary the location of the drop return from the middle of the table to the attacker's wide forehand.
- Have the feeder increase the speed of the forehand topspin.
- Have the feeder increase the amount of spin on the forehand topspin.

Success Check

- When executing the forehand flip, make sure your return cuts the forehand side line of the feeder's side of the table.
- When executing the forehand countertopspin, try to contact the ball as it rises or at the top of the bounce.

Score Your Success

Note how many times out of 10 tries you successfully executed all of the strokes in the pattern. Do not count misses by the feeder.

9 or 10 successful patterns = 10 points

7 or 8 successful patterns = 5 points

5 or 6 successful patterns = 1 point

Your score ____

Fourth-Ball Drill 1. *Fourth-Ball Counterattack Using Backhand Counter*

The focus of this drill is on counterattacking the feeder's opening attacking topspin. Perform the pattern 10 times; then reverse roles.

- First ball: The feeder serves a short or medium backspin to the attacker's backhand (figure 7.6).
- Second ball: The attacker pushes deep to the feeder's backhand, cutting the feeder's backhand side line if possible.

- Third ball: The feeder returns crosscourt using a backhand topspin return.
- Fourth ball: The attacker plays a strong backhand counterdrive to anywhere on the feeder's side of the table to try to win the point. If the ball is returned, the two play out the point.

To Increase Difficulty

- Have the feeder vary the locations of the backhand topspin to any point on the attacker's backhand half of the table.
- Have the feeder increase the speed of the returns.
- Have the feeder increase the amount of spin on the returns.

Success Check

- Try to cut the feeder's backhand side line of the table with your serve return.
- Execute your backhand counterdrive with speed (use second gear), hitting through the ball with little spin.

Score Your Success

Note how many times out of 10 tries you successfully executed all of the strokes in the pattern. Do not count misses by the feeder.

9 or 10 successful patterns = 10 points

7 or 8 successful patterns = 5 points

5 or 6 successful patterns = 1 point

Your score ___

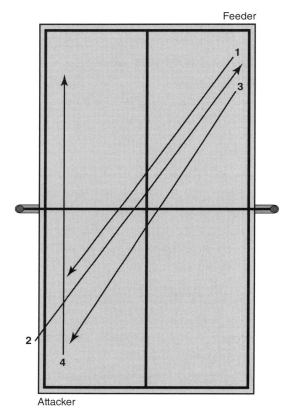

Figure 7.6 Ball placement during the fourth-ball counterattack using backhand counter drill.

Fourth-Ball Drill 2. *Fourth-Ball Attack With Backhand Flip and Forehand Countertopspin*

This drill focuses on the attacker's aggressive flip return of the serve. The attacker then anticipates a crosscourt return and pivots into the backhand corner to finish the point with a forehand topspin. Perform the pattern 10 times; then reverse roles.

- First ball: The feeder sends short mixed-spin serves to the attacker's backhand (figure 7.7).
- Second ball: The attacker returns crosscourt using a backhand flip return.

- Third ball: The feeder returns crosscourt using a backhand topspin return.
- Fourth ball: The attacker steps around the table and plays a strong forehand countertopspin return to anywhere on the feeder's side of the table to try to win the point. If the ball is returned, the two play out the point.

To Increase Difficulty

- Have the feeder use more spin on the serves and backhand topspin returns.

To Decrease Difficulty

- Have the feeder uses less spin on the serves and backhand topspin returns.

Success Check

- Make sure your backhand flip return cuts the feeder's backhand side line to help force a crosscourt return.
- Use the correct pivot footwork to move into position to use your forehand topspin.
- When executing the forehand countertopspin, contact the ball as it rises or at the top of the bounce.

Score Your Success

Note how many times out of 10 tries you successfully executed all of the strokes in the pattern. Do not count misses by the feeder.

9 or 10 successful patterns = 10 points

7 or 8 successful patterns = 5 points

5 or 6 successful patterns = 1 point

Your score ____

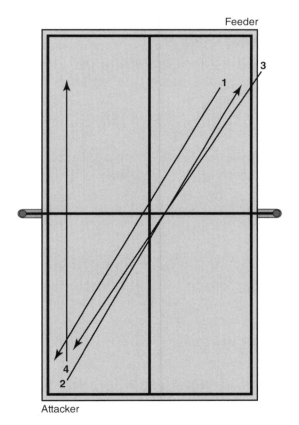

Figure 7.7 Ball placement during the fourth-ball attack with backhand flip and forehand countertopspin drill.

Fourth-Ball Drill 3. *Fourth-Ball Attack With Forehand Flip and Forehand Countertopspin*

This drill starts with the attacker directing a wide forehand flip that cuts the forehand side line to the feeder. The attacker then anticipates a crosscourt return and tries to finish the point with a forehand countertopspin. Perform the pattern 10 times; then reverse roles.

- First ball: The feeder sends a short mixed-spin serve to the attacker's forehand side (figure 7.8).

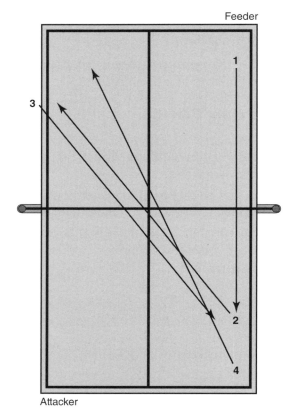

Figure 7.8 Ball placement for the fourth-ball attack with forehand flip and forehand countertopspin drill.

- Second ball: The attacker flips crosscourt, trying to place the ball so it cuts the side line of the table.
- Third ball: The feeder returns crosscourt using a forehand topspin return.
- Fourth ball: The attacker plays a strong forehand countertopspin to anywhere on the table to try to win the point. If the ball is returned, the two play out the point.

To Increase Difficulty

- Have the feeder add more spin to the serves and forehand topspin returns.

To Decrease Difficulty

- Have the feeder decrease the amount of spin on the serves and forehand topspin returns.

Success Check

- Make sure your forehand flip return cuts the feeder's forehand side line.
- When executing the forehand countertopspin, contact the ball as it rises or at the top of the bounce.

Score Your Success

Note how many times out of 10 tries you successfully executed all of the strokes in the pattern. Do not count misses by the feeder.

9 or 10 successful patterns = 10 points

7 or 8 successful patterns = 5 points

5 or 6 successful patterns = 1 point

Your score ____

Fourth-Ball Drill 4. *Fourth-Ball Attack With One Backhand Topspin and One Forehand Topspin*

This drill combines an aggressive backhand top-spin serve return with a pivot into the backhand corner so you can finish the point with a strong forehand topspin. Perform the pattern 10 times; then reverse roles.

- First ball: The feeder sends a long, fast, mixed-spin serve to the attacker's backhand (figure 7.9).
- Second ball: The attacker returns crosscourt using a backhand topspin return.

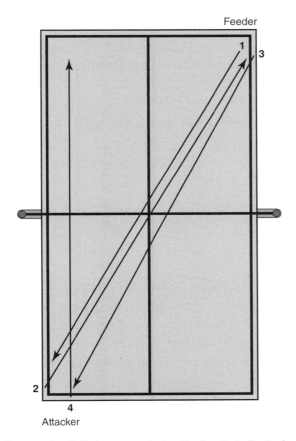

Figure 7.9 Ball placement during the fourth-ball attack with one backhand topspin and one forehand topspin drill.

- Third ball: The feeder returns crosscourt using a backhand counterdrive.
- Fourth ball: The attacker steps around the table and makes a strong forehand topspin to anywhere on the table to try to win the point. If the ball is returned, the two play out the point.

To Increase Difficulty

- Have the feeder vary the spin on the serves and increase the speed of the backhand counterdrives.

To Decrease Difficulty

- Have the feeder use the same deep serve and reduce the speed of the backhand counterdrive.

Success Check

- Make sure you are the proper arm-length's distance from the table when you receive serve.
- Try to cut the feeder's backhand side line with your serve return.
- Use the proper pivot footwork when moving into your backhand corner to play the forehand topspin.

Score Your Success

Note how many times out of 10 tries you successfully executed all of the strokes in the pattern. Do not count misses by the feeder.

9 or 10 successful patterns = 10 points

7 or 8 successful patterns = 5 points

5 or 6 successful patterns = 1 point

Your score ____

Fourth-Ball Drill 5. *Fourth-Ball Attack With Backhand Drop and Forehand Topspin*

In this drill, the attacker gives a short serve return to try to force a long push from the feeder. He then attacks the long push with his forehand. Perform the pattern 10 times; then reverse roles.

- First ball: The feeder sends a short backspin serve to the attacker's backhand (figure 7.10).
- Second ball: The attacker returns crosscourt with a short backhand drop return.

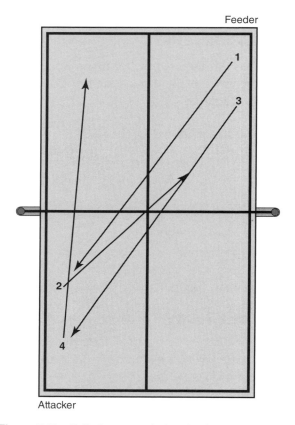

Figure 7.10 Ball placement during the fourth-ball attack with backhand drop and forehand topspin drill.

- Third ball: The feeder returns crosscourt using a backhand push return.
- Fourth ball: The attacker steps around the table and makes a strong forehand topspin return to anywhere on the table to try to win the point. If the ball is returned, the two play out the point.

To Increase Difficulty

- Have the feeder increase the amount of spin on the serve and push returns.

To Decrease Difficulty

- Have the feeder decrease the amount of spin on the serve and push returns.

Success Check

- Keep the ball low and short on your drop returns.
- After executing the drop return, recover to the ready position before the feeder makes the long push.
- When attacking the feeder's long push, contact the ball at the top of the bounce for maximum speed.

Score Your Success

Note how many times out of 10 tries you successfully executed all of the strokes in the pattern. Do not count misses by the feeder.

9 or 10 successful patterns = 10 points

7 or 8 successful patterns = 5 points

5 or 6 successful patterns = 1 point

Your score ___

Third-Ball Drill 1. *Third-Ball Attack With Short Serve Then Fast Topspin*

In this drill, the attacker serves short, trying to force a long push to attack. Perform the pattern 10 times; then reverse roles.

- First ball: The attacker sends a short serve to the feeder's backhand (figure 7.11).
- Second ball: The feeder returns crosscourt with a long push.

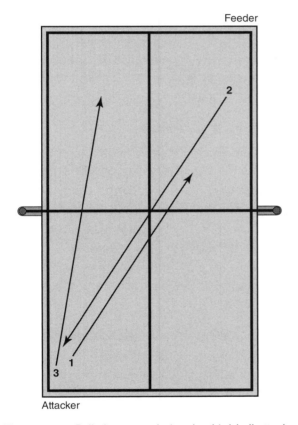

Figure 7.11 Ball placement during the third-ball attack with short serve then fast topspin drill.

- Third ball: The attacker steps around the table and makes a fast forehand topspin to anywhere on the feeder's side of the table to try to win the point. If the ball is returned, the two play out the point.

To Increase Difficulty

- Have the feeder vary the placement of the push returns within the backhand half of the attacker's side of the table.

To Decrease Difficulty

- Have the feeder direct all push returns to the same location.

Success Check

- Make sure your serves are short and low.
- After serving, return to the ready position before the feeder touches the ball.
- Move quickly into your backhand corner using the proper pivot footwork.
- When executing the forehand topspin against the push return, contact the ball at the top of the bounce.

Score Your Success

Note how many times out of 10 tries you successfully executed all of the strokes in the pattern. Do not count misses by the feeder.

9 or 10 successful patterns = 10 points

7 or 8 successful patterns = 5 points

5 or 6 successful patterns = 1 point

Your score ___

Third-Ball Drill 2. *Third-Ball Attack With Deep Serve Then Fast Topspin*

This drill combines a deep serve with a pivot into the forehand so you can attack the return with a forehand topspin. Perform the pattern 10 times; then reverse roles.

- First ball: The attacker sends a fast, deep serve to the feeder's backhand, trying to cut the side line of the table to force a crosscourt return (figure 7.12).
- Second ball: The feeder returns crosscourt using a backhand topspin.

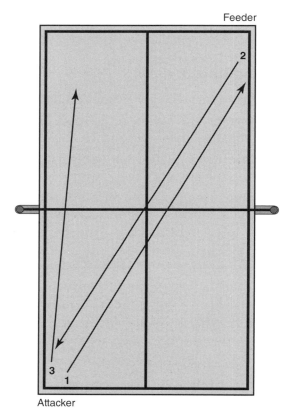

Feeder

Attacker

Figure 7.12 Ball placement during the third-ball attack with deep serve then fast topspin drill.

- Third ball: The feeder steps around the table and makes a fast forehand counterspin or counterdrive to anywhere on the feeder's side of the table to try to win the point. If the ball is returned, the two play out the point.

To Increase Difficulty

- Have the feeder increase the speed and the amount of spin on the backhand topspin returns.

To Decrease Difficulty

- Have the feeder decrease the speed and the amount of spin on the backhand topspin returns.

Success Check

- Make sure your serve is deep and fast and cuts the feeder's backhand side line.
- After serving, return to the ready position before the feeder touches the ball.
- Move quickly into your backhand corner using the proper pivot footwork.
- When executing the forehand counterspin or counterdrive, contact the ball at the top of the bounce.

Score Your Success

Note how many times out of 10 tries you successfully executed all of the strokes in the pattern. Do not count misses by the feeder.

9 or 10 successful patterns = 10 points

7 or 8 successful patterns = 5 points

5 or 6 successful patterns = 1 point

Your score ___

Third-Ball Drill 3. *Third-Ball Attack With Mid-Depth Serve Then Fast Topspin*

For this drill, the attacker must recognize the type of serve return the feeder is giving and adjust his attack accordingly. Perform the pattern 10 times; then reverse roles.

- First ball: The attacker gives a mid-depth serve to the feeder's backhand (figure 7.13).
- Second ball: The feeder returns crosscourt using a backhand flip or long push return.
- Third ball: The attacker steps around the table and makes a fast forehand topspin to

anywhere on the feeder's side of the table to try to win the point. If the ball is returned, the two play out the point.

To Increase Difficulty

- Have the feeder randomly mix the serve returns and vary the placement to anywhere on the attacker's backhand half of the table.

To Decrease Difficulty

- Have the feeder alternate between a push return and a flip return and return all balls to the same location.

Success Check

- After serving, return to the ready position before the feeder touches the ball.
- Move quickly into your backhand corner using the proper pivot footwork.
- When executing the forehand topspin or counterdrive, contact the ball at the top of the bounce.
- Remember to contact the ball slightly below the center of the ball's face against a backspin return and slightly above the center of the ball's face against a topspin return (flip).

Score Your Success

Note how many times out of 10 tries you successfully executed all of the strokes in the pattern. Do not count misses by the feeder.

9 or 10 successful patterns = 10 points

7 or 8 successful patterns = 5 points

5 or 6 successful patterns = 1 point

Your score ____

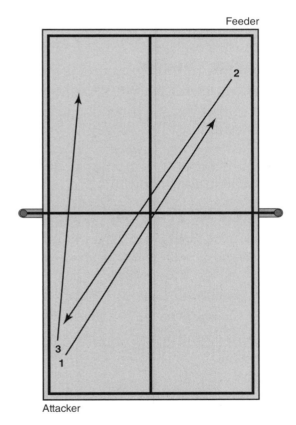

Feeder

Attacker

Figure 7.13 Ball placement during the third-ball attack with mid-depth serve then fast topspin drill.

Third-Ball Drill 4. *Third-Ball Attack With Short Serve and Flip*

In this drill, the attacker tries to win the point with a strong flip off the feeder's short drop serve return. Perform the pattern 10 times; then reverse roles.

- First ball: The attacker sends a short backspin serve to the feeder's forehand (figure 7.14).

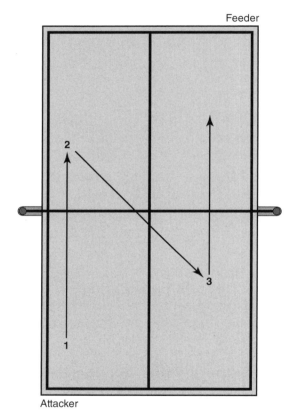

Feeder

Attacker

Figure 7.14 Ball placement during the third-ball attack with short serve and flip drill.

- Second ball: The feeder returns with a short drop to the attacker's forehand.
- Third ball: The attacker makes a forehand flip return to anywhere on the feeder's side of the table to try to win the point. If the ball is returned, the two play out the point.

To Increase Difficulty

- Have the feeder vary the location to anywhere on the attacker's forehand half of the table.

To Decrease Difficulty

- Have the feeder direct each serve to the same location.

Success Check

- Contact the ball at the top of the bounce.
- At contact, the racket arm should be moving upward.
- Your target areas are the deep corners, cutting the side lines if possible, or into the feeder's playing elbow.

Score Your Success

Note how many times out of 10 tries you successfully executed all of the strokes in the pattern. Do not count misses by the feeder.

9 or 10 successful patterns = 10 points

7 or 8 successful patterns = 5 points

5 or 6 successful patterns = 1 point

Your score ___

Second-Ball Drill 1. *Second-Ball Backhand Attack Against a Short Serve*

In this drill, the feeder gives a short serve to the attacker's backhand. The attacker then tries to win the point or gain the advantage by mixing returns between flips and drop returns to anywhere on the table. Perform the pattern 10 times; then reverse roles.

- First ball: The feeder sends a short serve to the attacker's backhand side (figure 7.15).

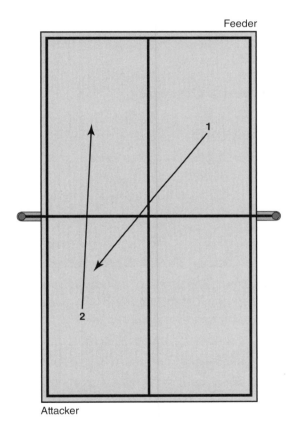

Feeder

Attacker

Figure 7.15 Ball placement during the second-ball backhand attack against a short serve drill.

- Second ball: The attacker tries to win the point with a flip or drop return to anywhere on the feeder's side of the table. If the ball is returned, the two play out the point.

To Increase Difficulty

- Have the feeder increase the amount of spin on the serves.

To Decrease Difficulty

- Have the feeder decrease the amount of spin on the serves.

Success Check

- When executing a flip return, contact the ball at the top of the bounce.
- When executing a drop return, contact the ball on the rise.
- Try to mix up drop and flip returns and their locations so that you force weak returns from the feeder.

Score Your Success

Note how many times out of 10 tries you successfully executed all of the strokes in the pattern. Do not count misses by the feeder.

9 or 10 successful patterns = 10 points

7 or 8 successful patterns = 5 points

5 or 6 successful patterns = 1 point

Your score ___

Second-Ball Drill 2. *Second-Ball Forehand Attack Against a Short Serve*

In this drill, the feeder gives a short serve to the attacker's forehand. The attacker then tries to win the point or gain the advantage by mixing returns between flips and drop returns to anywhere on the table. Perform the pattern 10 times; then reverse roles.

- First ball: The feeder sends a short backspin and sidespin serve to the attacker's forehand (figure 7.16).

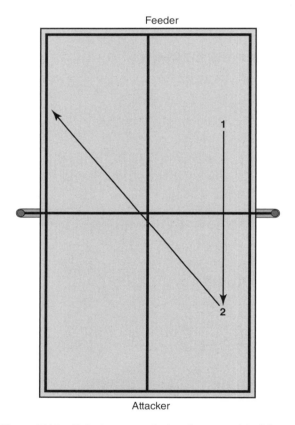

Feeder

Attacker

Figure 7.16 Ball placement during the second-ball forehand attack against a short serve drill.

- Second ball: The attacker tries to win the point with a forehand flip return or drop return to anywhere on the feeder's side of the table. If the ball is returned, the two play out the point.

To Increase Difficulty

- Have the feeder increase the amount of spin on the serves.

To Decrease Difficulty

- Have the feeder decrease the amount of spin on the serves.

Success Check

- When executing a flip return, contact the ball at the top of the bounce.
- When executing a drop return, contact the ball as it rises.
- Try to mix up drop and flip returns and their locations so that you force weak returns from the feeder.

Score Your Success

Note how many times out of 10 tries you successfully executed all of the strokes in the pattern. Do not count misses by the feeder.

9 or 10 successful patterns = 10 points

7 or 8 successful patterns = 5 points

5 or 6 successful patterns = 1 point

Your score ___

Second-Ball Drill 3. *Second-Ball Backhand Attack Against a Mid-Depth Serve*

In this drill, the attacker must recognize whether the serve will be long enough to attack with a backhand topspin stroke or whether a backhand flip will be needed. Perform the pattern 10 times; then reverse roles.

- First ball: The feeder sends a mid-depth serve to the attacker's backhand (figure 7.17).

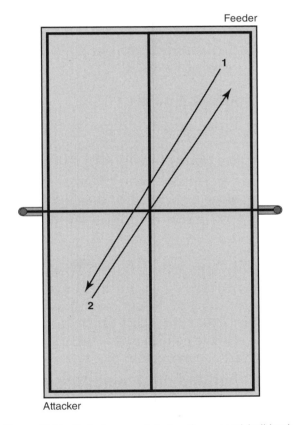

Figure 7.17 Ball placement during the second-ball backhand attack against a mid-depth serve drill.

- Second ball: The attacker tries to win the point with either a backhand flip or backhand topspin to anywhere on the feeder's side of the table. If the ball is returned, the two play out the point.

To Increase Difficulty

- Have the feeder change the type and amount of spin on the serves and also change the location to anywhere within the attacker's backhand side of the table.

To Decrease Difficulty

- Have the feeder always direct the serve to the same location.

Success Check

- Focus on returning the ball deep into the corners, cutting the side lines if possible, or into the elbow of the feeder's racket arm.
- Any serve that will come off the table before the second bounce on your side should be attacked using a full topspin stroke, not the flip.

Score Your Success

Note how many times out of 10 tries you successfully executed all of the strokes in the pattern. Count only your returns that land in the correct target areas (the corners or the feeder's playing elbow). Do not count misses by the feeder.

9 or 10 successful patterns = 10 points

7 or 8 successful patterns = 5 points

5 or 6 successful patterns = 1 point

Your score ____

Second-Ball Drill 4. *Second-Ball Forehand Attack Against a Mid-Depth Serve*

In this drill, the attacker must recognize whether the serve will be long enough to attack with a forehand topspin stroke or whether a forehand flip will be needed. Perform the pattern 10 times; then reverse roles.

- First ball: The feeder sends a mid-depth serve to the attacker's forehand (figure 7.18).

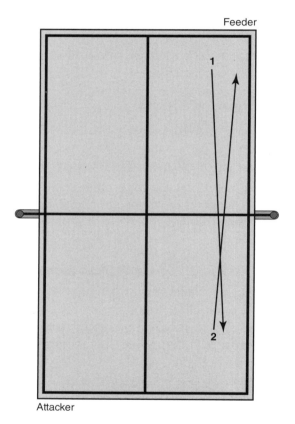

Feeder

Attacker

Figure 7.18 Ball placement during the second-ball forehand attack against a mid-depth serve drill.

- Second ball: The attacker tries to win the point with either a forehand flip or forehand topspin to anywhere on the feeder's side of the table. If the ball is returned, the two play out the point.

To Increase Difficulty

- Have the feeder change the type and amount of spin on the serves and also change the location to anywhere within the attacker's forehand side of the table.

To Decrease Difficulty

- Have the feeder always direct the serve to the same location.

Success Check

- Focus on returning the ball deep into the corners, cutting the side lines if possible, or into the elbow of the feeder's racket arm.
- Any serve that will come off the table before the second bounce on your side should be attacked using a full topspin stroke, not the flip.

Score Your Success

Note how many times out of 10 tries you successfully executed all of the strokes in the pattern. Count only your returns that land in the correct target areas (the corners or the feeder's playing elbow). Do not count misses by the feeder.

9 or 10 successful patterns = 10 points

7 or 8 successful patterns = 5 points

5 or 6 successful patterns = 1 point

Your score ___

Second-Ball Drill 5. *Second-Ball Backhand Attack Against a Deep Serve*

In this drill, the feeder sends deep serves to the attacker's backhand. The attacker returns the serve using a backhand topspin, trying to win the point outright or force an error from the feeder. Perform the pattern 10 times; then reverse roles.

- First ball: The feeder sends a long, fast serve to the attacker's backhand (figure 7.19).

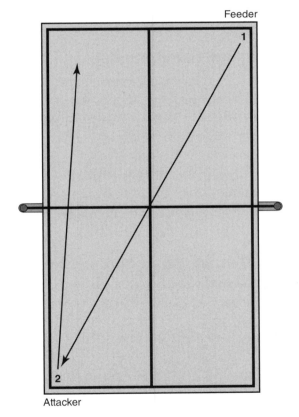

Figure 7.19 Ball placement during the second-ball backhand attack against a deep serve drill.

- Second ball: The attacker tries to win the point with a backhand topspin to anywhere on the feeder's side of the table. If the ball is returned, the two play out the point.

To Increase Difficulty

- Have the feeder vary the types of serve and the amount of spin on the serves.

To Decrease Difficulty

- Have the feeder always use the same serve.

Success Check

- Place your returns deep into the corners, cutting the side lines if possible, or direct your returns into the feeder's playing elbow.
- After playing the topspin return, recover quickly to the ready position.
- Try to vary the amount of topspin on your returns.
- Try to keep your serve returns low over the net.

Score Your Success

Note how many times out of 10 tries you successfully executed all of the strokes in the pattern. Count only your returns that land in the correct target areas (the corners or the feeder's playing elbow). Do not count misses by the feeder.

9 or 10 successful patterns = 10 points

7 or 8 successful patterns = 5 points

5 or 6 successful patterns = 1 point

Your score ___

Second-Ball Drill 6. *Second-Ball Forehand Attack Against a Deep Serve*

In this drill, the feeder sends deep serves to the attacker's forehand. The attacker returns the serve using a forehand topspin, trying to win the point outright or force an error from the feeder. Perform the pattern 10 times; then reverse roles.

- First ball: The feeder sends a long, fast serve to the attacker's forehand (figure 7.20).

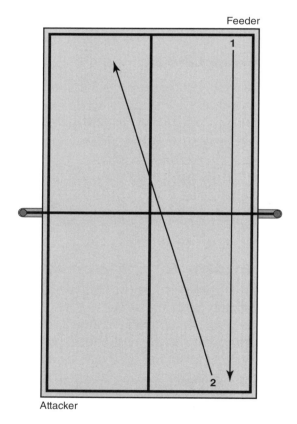

Feeder

Attacker

Figure 7.20 Ball placement during the second-ball forehand attack against a deep serve drill.

- Second ball: The attacker tries to win the point with a forehand topspin to anywhere on the feeder's side of the table. If the ball is returned, the two play out the point.

To Increase Difficulty

- Have the feeder vary the types of serve and the amount of spin on the serves.

To Decrease Difficulty

- Have the feeder always use the same serve.

Success Check

- Place returns deep into the corners, cutting the side lines if possible, or direct your returns into the feeder's playing elbow.
- After playing the topspin return, recover quickly to the ready position.
- Try to vary the amount of topspin on your returns.
- Try to keep your serve returns low over the net.

Score Your Success

Note how many times out of 10 tries you successfully executed all of the strokes in the pattern. Count only your returns that land in the correct target areas (the corners or the feeder's playing elbow). Do not count misses by the feeder.

9 or 10 successful patterns = 10 points

7 or 8 successful patterns = 5 points

5 or 6 successful patterns = 1 point

Your score ___

First-Ball Drill. *Serve and Attack Games*

In this drill, the focus is on using the serve as aggressively as possible to set up the point. Try to mix up the depth, placement, and spin on your serve to force your opponent to give you an easy return to attack.

The attacker serves and tries to win the point on the serve, on the third-ball attack, or on the fifth-ball attack. The feeder also tries to win the point. The feeder may use any type of return and placement. Any point lasting longer than five strokes belongs to the feeder. Play 10 points, with the attacker serving every point; then switch roles.

To Increase Difficulty

- The attacker must win the point with either the serve or the first attack (the third ball).

Success Check

- Try to mix up the types of serves you use and their locations.
- Use your strongest strokes as quickly as possible in the point.
- Pay attention to the placement of your returns.

Score Your Success

Score yourself based on how many points you won as the attacker.

More than 7 points won = 10 points

5 to 7 points won = 5 points

3 to 5 points won = 1 point

Your score ___

SUCCESS SUMMARY OF USING THE FIVE-BALL TRAINING SYSTEM

In this step, you learned to use the five-ball training system to practice common patterns. This method of practice allows you to focus on one of the first five strokes of a point. As you learn to play points, you will develop your own personal style of play. The five-ball training system should be a regular part of training for players at all levels. Your game will never outgrow the need to improve the quality of your individual patterns of play.

To see whether you are ready to move on to step 8, add up your drill scores. If you scored at least 160 points, you are ready to move on to step 8. If not, you need more practice.

Fifth-Ball Drills

1. Fifth Ball With Two Forehand Topspins   ___ out of 10

2. Fifth Ball With Two Backhand Topspins   ___ out of 10

3. Fifth Ball With One Backhand Topspin and One Forehand
   Topspin   ___ out of 10

4. Fifth Ball With Backhand Counterdrive and Forehand Topspin   ___ out of 10

5. Fifth Ball With Forehand Flip Return and Forehand
   Countertopspin   ___ out of 10

(continued)

(continued)

Fourth-Ball Drills

1.	Fourth-Ball Counterattack Using Backhand Counter	___ out of 10
2.	Fourth-Ball Attack With Backhand Flip and Forehand Countertopspin	___ out of 10
3.	Fourth-Ball Attack With Forehand Flip and Forehand Countertopspin	___ out of 10
4.	Fourth-Ball Attack With One Backhand Topspin and One Forehand Topspin	___ out of 10
5.	Fourth-Ball Attack With Backhand Drop and Forehand Topspin	___ out of 10

Third-Ball Drills

1.	Third-Ball Attack With Short Serve Then Fast Topspin	___ out of 10
2.	Third-Ball Attack With Deep Serve Then Fast Topspin	___ out of 10
3.	Third-Ball Attack With Mid-Depth Serve Then Fast Topspin	___ out of 10
4.	Third-Ball Attack With Short Serve and Flip	___ out of 10

Second-Ball Drills

1.	Second-Ball Backhand Attack Against a Short Serve	___ out of 10
2.	Second-Ball Forehand Attack Against a Short Serve	___ out of 10
3.	Second-Ball Backhand Attack Against a Mid-Depth Serve	___ out of 10
4.	Second-Ball Forehand Attack Against a Mid-Depth Serve	___ out of 10
5.	Second-Ball Backhand Attack Against a Deep Serve	___ out of 10
6.	Second-Ball Forehand Attack Against a Deep Serve	___ out of 10

First-Ball Drill

1.	Serve and Attack Games	___ out of 10

Total   ___ *out of 210*

After working with the five-ball system of training for a while, you will notice that certain strokes and patterns of play are quickly becoming personal favorites. The next step in your development as a player is to incorporate these strengths into your own style of play. Step 8 introduces the basic styles of players found in the game and the tactics they use in match play.

Understanding Styles of Play and Tactics

In step 7, you learned to combine strokes into whole points by using the five-ball training system. As you reach this point in your development, your own personal style begins to come together. This step introduces the seven basic styles of play and guides you through the process of developing your own style. Basic tactics of play are also introduced.

SEVEN PLAYING STYLES

The seven basic styles of play are pips-out penholder, counterdriver, close-to-the-table defender, attacking chopper, mid-distance looper, power looper, and all-around attacker. Most players develop styles that are a combination of two of these styles.

One of the most important decisions you will make is selecting a personal style of play. Consider these three keys when developing your own style:

1. What are your strongest strokes? Build your style around getting your strengths into the game as quickly and as often as possible.

2. What style do you enjoy playing? You will not be successful with your game unless you enjoy the style you play.

3. What speed is required for the style? Three types of speed are required in table tennis: hand speed (how quick are your hand-to-ball movements?), foot speed (how fast can you move around the court?), and ball speed or power (how much power can you generate on your strokes?).

As you read through the style descriptions, you should be able to find one that matches the game you are beginning to play. Most players have one dominant style and a secondary style they use in emergencies.

Pips-Out Penholder

A player who uses this style of play uses the penhold grip and short pips-out rubber on the forehand side of the racket. The pips-out penholder generally stands within 3 feet (about 1 m) of the table. On all strokes, the contact point is as early as possible either at the top of the bounce or as the ball is rising. This is a forehand-dominated style in which the player exhibits a strong, quick pivot move to use the forehand from the backhand side. The pips-out penholder wants to end points quickly and is a master of playing the ball off the bounce. This quick return of the ball takes away the opponent's time to react, creating time pressure and forcing many errors. This style of play was made famous by many Chinese world champions in the 1960s through the 1990s and is still common today. The development of the reverse pen-hold backhand stroke has revitalized this style of play and mostly eliminated the original backhand weaknesses of this style.

Speed Elements

Hand speed = high

Foot speed = high

Power = high

Traditional Strengths

- Quick pivot from the backhand corner to use the forehand.
- Strong forehand kills.
- Good forehand topspin against long backspin balls.
- Punch blocks from the backhand side.
- Good short game.
- Excellent serve–return game.
- Very quick, off-the-bounce returns to give the opponent very little time to react.
- Smooth transition from forehand to backhand with no switch point weaknesses.

Traditional Weaknesses

- Weak return of long serves with the backhand.
- Weak backhand block against higher-bouncing loops.
- When forced wide to the forehand, a player who uses this style may have difficulty recovering and protecting the backhand side.
- Weak backhand attacks against long backspin returns.

These backhand weaknesses may disappear if the player can use the reverse pen-hold backhand stroke.

Counterdriver

This style of player is often referred to as a *wall*. A player who uses this style plays close to the table and redirects the opponent's speed and spin against him. The main strokes are blocks and counterdrives, and their placement and consistency often force the opponent to make errors. This style mostly uses topspin simply as a means to get into a counterdriving rally and often lacks any real finishing power. Although this is a successful style at the local tournament level, it is rarely seen at the professional level.

Speed Elements

Hand speed = high

Foot speed = medium

Power = low

Traditional Strengths

- Good hand speed and touch on blocks.
- Strong backhand block and counterdrive.
- Player rarely makes a simple mistake.
- Ability to open up angles and force opponent out of position.
- Ability to control the speed of play by clever counter and block variations and exact placement.

Traditional Weaknesses

- Lack of any real power.
- Opponent can direct balls wide to the forehand.
- Difficulty attacking backspin with the backhand.
- Difficulty returning higher-topspin balls that are directed to the middle or backhand side.

Close-to-the-Table Defender

This style is built around a chop block or sidespin block that is executed from close to the table. Players using this style most often use combination rackets with long pips or antispin on one side and inverted rubber or short pips-out rubber on the other. These players use off-speed blocks to force weak topspin shots or push returns from their opponents. They then attack these returns with well-placed drives or topspin shots. The close-to-the-table defender is a master of placement but lacks real finishing power. This style is very popular with older athletes who have good hand skills but lack mobility and need to slow down the opponent's game to be effective.

Speed Elements

Hand speed = high

Foot speed = low

Power = medium

Traditional Strengths

- Very consistent chop blocks executed from close to the table.
- Excellent serve–receive game.
- Very accurate forehand drives.
- Excellent short game that uses pushes and drop shots.
- Ability to absorb opponent's strong opening shots.

Traditional Weaknesses

- No real power.
- Opponent can direct high, looping balls directed to the backhand.
- Opponent can direct hard balls toward the wide forehand.
- No-spin serves and pushes often force errors.

Attacking Chopper

The attacking chopper can best be thought of as an attacker who uses backspin to set up his attacking shots. Players of this style most often use long pips on one side of the racket and inverted rubber on the other and flip the racket to produce great variations in defense and attack. Modern attacking choppers usually have powerful forehand loops and kills and a strong backhand chopping game. They attack strongly

any weak return by the opponent as well as any third-ball opportunity.

Since the advent of the 40-millimeter ball, the attacking chopper style has evolved into one in which almost every forehand return is attacked and backhand returns are chopped with very heavy-spin returns from a position somewhat closer to the table than in past years. Most often, players who use this style of play choose long-pimpled rubber for the backhand side of the blade to aid in chopping, and inverted rubber for the forehand side to permit topspin attacks.

This style of play continues to be popular at the professional level, but the extreme physical demands of the style make it relatively rare at the local tournament level. Because players of this style must learn both offensive and defensive strokes, this style of play takes longer to learn than most.

Speed Elements

Hand speed = high

Foot speed = high

Power = high

Traditional Strengths

- Great variation of strokes and spin puts opponents under a lot of pressure.
- Strong forehand drives or kills.
- Strong third-ball attacks.
- Good movement and physical ability.
- Strong backspin returns require opponents to exert a great amount of energy to continually attack. This can lead to fatigue and force opponents to make errors.

Traditional Weaknesses

- This style of player can become impatient and attack the wrong ball.
- Footwork problems are common when switching from chopping to topspin attack shots.
- The attacking chopper's defense may not stand up under pressure.
- Too many options may result in some indecisiveness under pressure.

Mid-Distance Looper

Players who use this style prefer to play at mid-range from the table, 3 to 8 feet (around 1 to 2.4 m). They use longer topspin strokes that carry a lot of power, and are equally strong with both forehand and backhand. A mid-distance looper loops from both wings when playing another attacker. Against a defensive player, she will step around and use more forehand topspin strokes.

The introduction of the 40-millimeter ball has had a major impact on this style of play. The resulting loss of spin caused by the larger ball has forced this style of player to become more fit and powerful to survive. Gone are the days when players using this style would defeat opponents by building up spin with each loop. Now, this style builds up speed with each loop. In today's game, this style is much more dynamic with even faster point-winning loops. This style is often preferred by taller athletes because it allows them to take full advantage of their reach and size.

Speed Elements

Hand speed = medium

Foot speed = medium

Power = high

Traditional Strengths

- Equal power from both sides.
- Very strong opening shot against backspin.
- Very comfortable in exchanging topspin drives with opponents.
- Strong lateral movement.

Traditional Weaknesses

- These players often lack a flat kill shot.
- Weak in and out movement.
- Opponent can place short balls to the forehand.
- Weak counterdrives when close to the table.

Power Looper

Power loopers generally stay close to the table and try to play all balls at the top of the bounce for maximum speed on returns. This is a forehand-dominated style in which the player exhibits a strong, quick pivot move to use the forehand from the backhand side. Players who use this style try to end points as quickly as possible by using fast, topspin drives. They often have both an outstanding slow loop and a fast loop kill from the forehand side. Power loopers can open with a backhand topspin but normally do not win many points with the backhand. On occasion, players who use this style move back into mid-distance and execute counterloops with the forehand. Power loopers have won many world championships and can be found at all levels of play.

Players of this style have generally done well with the move to the 40-millimeter ball. Their main adjustment has been to develop a more forward loop stroke, taking the ball a little farther in front of their bodies. This puts more emphasis on the forward speed than on the spin of their power loops.

Speed Elements

Hand speed = high

Foot speed = high

Power = high

Traditional Strengths

- Quick pivot from the backhand corner to use the forehand.
- Powerful, point-winning forehand topspins.
- Both strong slow and fast loops from the forehand.
- Solid opening backhand topspins.
- Solid backhand counterdrives.
- Good short game.
- Excellent serve–return game.

Traditional Weaknesses

- Balls may be directed toward the player's middle.
- Balls may be directed wide to the power looper's forehand.
- In and out movement.

- Lack of a backhand countertopspin stroke.
- Slow, heavy-spin loops may be directed toward the power looper's backhand.

All-Around Attacker

This is one of the newest styles in the evolution of the modern game. The all-around attacker typically exhibits great hands, a wide variety of attacking strokes that he can execute with almost equal strength from both sides, and the ability to adapt his game to attack the opponent's weaknesses.

This all-around attacker is equally comfortable generating powerful strokes and simply redirecting the opponent's power. Players of this style can produce a wide variety of topspin attacking shots from any position or distance from the table.

Speed Elements

Hand speed = high

Foot speed = medium-high

Power = medium-high

Traditional Strengths

- Strong first attacking strokes from either backhand or forehand.
- Ability to produce a great deal of variation in attacks.
- Ability to control the ball at high rates of speed.
- Use of sidespin to control the ball and create greater angles for opponents to cover.
- Plays well when in the lead.

Traditional Weaknesses

- Can become confused as to which of the many techniques to use, especially when losing.
- Can be lured into playing too softly and not being aggressive enough to finish a point.
- Often lacks a single, hard finishing shot (flat kill) against balls at medium height.

Tactics Drill 1. Select Your Playing Style

This exercise will help you select your style of play. Answer the following questions:

1. What two strokes do you count on most to win points?

2. What kind of hand speed, foot speed, and power (ball speed) can you generate? Rate yourself low, medium, medium-high, or high.

3. Who do you know who demonstrates each of the styles described in this step? Use the descriptions of the seven basic styles to identify a player you play with who fits each description. If you cannot find an example of a person who uses a style from within your own playing group, try to find one from the many videos available for free on the Internet. List a player who is an example of each style:

Pips-out penholder _____

Counterdriver _____

Close-to-the-table defender _____

Attacking chopper _____

Mid-distance looper _____

Power looper _____

All-around attacker _____

After answering these questions, you should have some idea of the style of play you currently have or would like to develop. Remember, your own style will probably be a blend of two of these basic styles. Your dominant style, or A style, is the one you will try to play most often. Your B style will be the one you go to when you need to mix up your tactics. List your styles here:

My A style _____

My B style _____

To Decrease Difficulty

- Ask your practice partners or coaches which style of play they think best suits your abilities.

Success Check

- Take the time to find players who exemplify each style of play and study their strengths and weaknesses.

- Make sure the style of play you pick for yourself not only fits your abilities but is also one you enjoy playing.

Score Your Success

Identify your A style = 5 points
Identify your B style = 5 points
Your score ___

BASIC TACTICS

One of the most difficult skills for the average player to learn is match strategy. There are several reasons for this. Forming a match strategy requires the ability to focus on what your opponent is doing. This can be difficult when your own strokes are not sound. It requires a great deal of experience to realize what strategies work against various styles. Finally, it is hard to find much in writing regarding match tactics. This is largely due to the complexity and individuality of the issue. With all this is mind, how does the developing athlete begin to develop his or her own match tactics? Here is a simple way to get started.

To begin, you need to understand the four ways to win a point: using power, setting traps for the opponent, using special techniques, and creating time pressure.

Every time you begin a point during a match, you should have an idea of which of these methods you want to use. Your own primary method of winning points will depend on your style. What is important is that you play each point with purpose and are aware of what is or is not working for you. Never change a winning strategy, but always change a losing strategy.

Using Power

A powerful stroke can best be described as any stroke that can generate enough speed to penetrate your opponent's defense. It is important to understand clearly which of your strokes has the potential to end the point. You also need to know on what kind of return from your opponent

you can best execute this stroke. Using power to win a point is often considered the ultimate technique because often an opponent has no answer to a ball that is hit hard enough.

Setting Traps

Setting traps to win points is about forcing your opponent to commit errors as you vary the speed, spin, height, and placement of your returns.

Here are some common examples of traps you can set for your opponent:

- Change the amount of spin on your returns. Hit one with light spin and the next with heavy spin.
- Change the height of your topspin returns.
- Play a short return followed by a long return.
- Play a slow return followed by a fast return.
- Move your returns from corner to corner.
- Attack your opponent's playing elbow, the switch point between the backhand and forehand if your opponent uses a shakehands grip.

Against a player who uses long pips or antirubber on one side of the racket, direct serves and pushes that have little or no spin to that side to force errors. Also, higher, light-topspin returns to that side will be difficult for the player to attack.

More games are won by simply making fewer unforced errors than by any other tactical method.

Using Special Techniques

A special technique is any stroke or tactic that is special to your style of play and that your opponent may not have seen often. This can include the use of a combination racket (one with different types of rubbers on either side), special serves, or unique shots that your opponent is not comfortable returning.

Although not all players have something unique about their games, it is always a good idea to try to cultivate an unusual stroke that your opponent may not have seen very often. The more adjustments you can force your opponent to make, the more errors he is likely to make.

Creating Time Pressure

To create time pressure, you must play the ball early off the bounce to force your opponent to execute her strokes at a quicker pace than she may be comfortable with. This technique often is used by players who play a close-to-the-table attacking style of play. Through the use of this tactic, you take away the time your opponent needs to set up for her strokes, which can force weak returns and errors. In general, this technique is ineffective against players who use long pips on one side of the racket because this type of rubber slows down their returns.

As you begin to understand your personal style and its strengths and weaknesses, you will begin to develop your own tactical plans for playing against each of the seven basic styles of play. Just remember, always start each point with a plan. At the lower levels of the game, your opponent may have a clear weakness. If so, once you discover it, keep playing into it until your opponent is able to make a correction. As your playing level increases, you will find that higher-level opponents can make adjustments to your strategy as the game progresses. Often, you will need to make several changes to your tactics throughout the game to keep better players guessing about what is coming next.

Tactics Drill 2. *Identify Your Strengths*

Prepare yourself for match play by asking yourself how you can use your best shots to win points by using power, setting traps, using special techniques, or creating time pressure. Answer the following questions to create your own match strategy:

1. What are your four best power strokes? Note the kinds of returns you like to hit these power strokes against.

2. What are your four favorite traps to set for opponents?

3. What unique or special techniques do you have?

4. What strokes can you execute that could put your opponent under time pressure?

To Decrease Difficulty

- Ask your practice partners or coaches for feedback on each of these questions.

Success Check

- If possible, try to videotape some of your games with your practice partners to see whether you are really winning points by the methods you have listed.

Score Your Success

Identify your strengths = 5 points

Use a game plan based on your strengths in competition = 5 points

Your score ___

Tactics Drill 3. *Develop a Tactical Plan*

This drill will help you develop a simple tactical plan for playing against each of the basic styles. Remember that every opponent is unique. Often, you will need to modify your tactics to fit your opponent and the situation. Step 11 addresses how to scout your opponent before a match.

Start by looking over your answers to the questions in tactics drills 1 and 2. Considering your own style of play, list four ways to win a point against each style of play and rank them in order from 1 (most important tactic) to 4 (least important tactic). Remember, your answers should be based on how you would approach playing each style. Your responses to this exercise should help you develop your basic tactical plan against each style of play. After completing this drill, have your practice partners look over your answers and provide feedback.

1. Pips-out penholder

2. Counterdriver

3. Close-to-the-table defender

4. Attacking chopper

5. Mid-distance looper

6. Power looper

7. All-around attacker

To Decrease Difficulty

- Have a coach or an experienced tournament player who is familiar with your game look over your answers and provide feedback.

Success Check

- Make sure you have a plan to play against each style of player.
- Try out your tactical plan against your practice partners.
- Update and change your plan as your skills improve.

Score Your Success

Develop a tactical plan against all seven styles of play = 10 points

Your score ___

SUCCESS SUMMARY OF UNDERSTANDING STYLES OF PLAY AND TACTICS

Learning to develop and successfully implement match strategy is the real challenge of table tennis. The ability to figure out your opponent's game and implement a winning strategy against it takes a great deal of tournament experience. Consider video recording your matches to help you analyze both your style of play and your tactics and those of your opponents.

Add up your drill scores. To be ready to move on to step 9, complete the three drills in this step and ask a coach or experienced player to review your answers. Use their feedback to fine-tune your plan before you move on to step 9.

Tactics Drills

1. Select Your Playing Style   ___ out of 10

2. Identify Your Strengths   ___ out of 10

3. Develop a Tactical Plan   ___ out of 10

Total   ___ *out of 30*

Players of all styles need to master the basic strokes. Step 9 describes more advanced stroke techniques that you can choose from to complete your own personal style of play.

Playing Intermediate Strokes

This step describes a number of more advanced stroke techniques. You do not need to learn all of these strokes. Rather, you should select which of these strokes will help you finish developing your own style of play.

USING ADVANCED BLOCKS

The word *block* refers to a very short stroke used against an attacking stroke to simply ricochet the ball back to the opponent, using the opponent's speed and spin against him.

At the higher levels of the game, the basic backhand block is not used often, if at all. It simply is not a strong enough return to keep an opponent from finishing the point. The forehand block is even more rarely used because advanced players take every opportunity to attack any ball coming to their forehand side. For this reason, only the backhand block variations will be addressed. However, several more aggressive backhand blocks can be very effective. Players of every style of play can benefit from learning the variations of this stroke. Look over the block variations that follow and choose at least one to learn.

Topspin Block

The topspin block is best when used against a medium-fast topspin return. To execute this stroke, use your forearm to make the racket brush up on the ball to produce a fast topspin return. This is a shorter version of the full backhand off-the-bounce topspin that uses only the forearm and wrist snap to add some spin to the block. This stroke can be executed with either a shake-hands (figure 9.1) or pen-hold grip (figure 9.2). Although this stroke can be produced with the traditional pen-hold backhand, it works much better with the modern reverse pen-hold backhand grip.

Three Basic Elements for the Topspin Block

How to touch the ball = with friction contact

When to touch the ball = as the ball is rising

Where to touch the ball = toward the top of the ball

From the ready position, move into a position so that the ball is centered in the backhand triangle as discussed in step 2 (page 19). The backswing is very short, bringing the racket back toward the body about parallel to the end line of the table. The racket face is closed. Because you are not providing power to the ball, play this stroke with the foot on your racket side behind your other foot. Move your forearm forward to bring the racket to the ball and contact the ball as it rises. At contact, the forearm moves forward and the wrist brushes up to add more topspin to the return, making friction contact. Use a short follow-through and recover to a ready position.

Figure 9.1   Topspin Block With Shake-Hands Grip

BACKSWING

1. Move so ball is in center of backhand triangle
2. Bring racket back parallel to end line
3. Racket is in closed position

a

CONTACT

1. Contact ball as it rises
2. Racket contacts ball above center of ball's face
3. Wrist brushes up on contact

b

FOLLOW-THROUGH

1. Forearm moves slightly forward
2. Wrist finishes higher, indicating application of topspin
3. Relax playing arm and recover to ready position

c

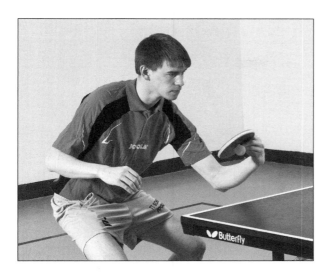

Figure 9.2 Contact during a topspin block with the player using a reverse pen-hold grip.

Punch Block

The punch block (figure 9.3) is best against a slower, heavy topspin return. It works well with either the shake-hands or pen-hold grip, either traditional or reverse. Begin the stroke the same way as you did the basic block. Then, on contact, quickly push your elbow forward and snap your wrist forward to add force to the ball. This produces a fast, very flat return with little spin that is difficult to re-topspin. The punch block is an excellent return against an opponent's opening topspin stroke and will often stop his attack.

Three Basic Elements for the Punch Block

How to touch the ball = maximum force contact with downward pressure

When to touch the ball = at the top of the bounce

Where to touch the ball = toward the top of the ball

From the ready position, move into a position so that the ball is centered in the backhand triangle as discussed in step 2 (page 19). Use a short backswing to bring the racket toward the body about parallel to the end line of the table. The racket face is closed. Usually this stroke is played with the foot on the racket side behind the other foot. Move your forearm forward to bring the racket to the ball and contact the ball as it rises. At contact, the forearm moves forward quickly and the wrist snaps forward, making force contact with the ball. The racket contacts the ball above the center of the ball's face. Add force to the ball forward and down. Whether you use a shake-hands or pen-hold grip, this stroke is executed almost identically. However, if you use the traditional pen-hold grip, use less wrist and push forward more aggressively with your forearm on contact. Use a short follow-through and recover to the ready position.

Misstep
On your topspin block, you do not produce enough topspin on the return.
Correction
Use more of your wrist at contact with the ball to increase the racket acceleration.

Figure 9.3   Punch Block With Shake-Hands Grip

BEGINNING POSITION

1. Move so ball is in center of backhand triangle
2. Bring racket back parallel to end line
3. Racket is in closed position

a

CONTACT

1. Contact ball as it rises
2. Racket contacts ball above center of ball's face
3. Forearm pushes forward at contact
4. Wrist snaps forward and down

b

FOLLOW-THROUGH

1. Forearm moves forward slightly
2. Wrist snaps forward and down, indicating a flat return with little spin
3. Relax playing arm and recover to ready position

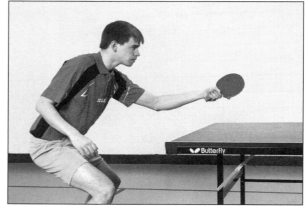

c

Misstep

On your punch block, the ball keeps going long.

Correction

Push both forward and down when contacting the ball.

Sidespin Block

The sidespin block is often used against a strong topspin attack as a safe way to return the ball. Adding some sidespin to your block returns will cause your returns to break sideways on contact with the table. This type of return can often force errors from an opponent. Adding some sidespin to your block also causes your return to travel a curved path rather than a straight path. Because a curved path is longer than a straight one, you have more room to hit the table. This makes the sidespin block a safer return than the basic block when facing a strong topspin attack. Although a sidespin block can be executed with any grip, players who use the shake-hands and reverse pen-hold grips often find the right sidespin block (figure 9.4) easier to execute. Players who use traditional pen-hold backhands more often use the left sidespin block.

Three Basic Elements for the Sidespin Block

How to touch the ball = mixed friction and force contact

When to touch the ball = as the ball is rising

Where to touch the ball = on the right or left side and toward the top of the ball

From the ready position, move into a position so that the ball is centered in the backhand triangle as discussed in step 2 (page 19). Use a short backswing to bring the racket back toward your body about parallel to the end line of the table. The racket face is closed. Usually, a right-handed player executes this stroke with the right foot behind the left. Move your forearm forward to bring the racket to the ball and contact the ball as it rises. At contact, your forearm quickly moves forward to your right. The racket contacts the ball above the center of the ball's face and toward the right side of the ball. If you want more sidespin, use more friction contact. The racket finishes to the right of the body. To use left sidespin, contact the ball on the left side (figure 9.5) and finish with the racket on the left side of the body. Use a short follow-through and recover to a ready position.

<table>
<tr><td>Figure 9.4</td><td>Right Sidespin Block With Shake-Hands Grip</td></tr>
</table>

BEGINNING POSITION

1. Move so ball is in center of backhand triangle when it bounces
2. Bring racket parallel to end line
3. Racket is in closed position

a

(continued)

Figure 9.4 *(continued)*

CONTACT

1. Forearm moves forward to bring racket to ball
2. Racket contacts ball above center of ball's face and toward right side of ball
3. Wrist snaps and rotates to right, imparting right sidespin
4. Racket head points up

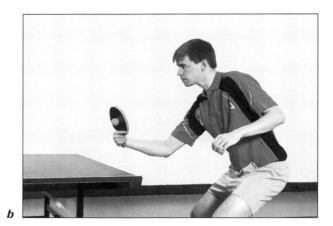

b

FOLLOW-THROUGH

1. Forearm moves forward slightly
2. Racket finishes on right side of body
3. Relax playing arm and recover to ready position

c

Figure 9.5 Left sidespin block with player using a traditional pen-hold grip.

 Misstep

Your sidespin block lacks sidespin.

Correction

To produce a right sidespin block, make sure you start your racket to the left of the ball and swing left to right.

Chop Block

The chop block variation (figure 9.6) is used to slow down your return to an opponent. When used with long pips or antispin rubbers, this return can produce a great deal of backspin. When executed with inverted rubbers, its main purpose is to change the speed of the return. This is a staple return for the close-to-the-table defender. Either a pen-hold or shake-hands grip can be used.

This stroke is executed with a somewhat closed blade. At contact with the ball, the wrist is used to move the racket downward. The racket has little or no forward motion.

Three Basic Elements for the Chop Block

How to touch the ball = friction contact

When to touch the ball = as the ball is rising

Where to touch the ball = above the center of the ball with the racket moving downward

From the ready position, move so that, when it bounces, the ball is centered in the backhand triangle as discussed in step 2 (page 19). There is almost no backswing with this stroke. The racket starts above the ball in a closed position. Typically, this stroke is played with the right foot behind the left (in right-handed players). Contact the ball very soon after the bounce with a short downward (not forward) motion of the forearm and wrist. The racket contacts the ball above the center of the ball's face with friction contact. The racket finishes in a downward position and directly in front of the body. Use a short follow-through and recover to a ready position.

The racket angle at contact will depend on the type of rubber being used. With long pips and antispin rubbers, the racket face can be more open at contact. With inverted rubbers, the racket face should be more closed at contact.

Figure 9.6 Chop Block With Shake-Hands Grip

LIMITED BACKSWING

1. Move to center ball in backhand triangle
2. Racket is close to where ball will bounce
3. Racket is in closed position and slightly higher than ball

a

CONTACT

1. Forearm moves forward and down to bring racket to ball
2. Racket contacts ball above center of ball's face
3. Racket moves down to ball
4. Wrist brushes down to impart backspin and make friction contact

b

FOLLOW-THROUGH

1. Forearm moves down, not forward
2. Wrist snaps down to impart backspin
3. Racket finishes low and directly in front of body
4. Relax playing arm and recover to ready position

c

Misstep

On your chop block, the return keeps going long.

Correction

Close your blade more and let your wrist move down at contact.

Intermediate Strokes Drill 1. *Alternating Backhand Counterdrives and Topspin Block Returns*

Have your practice partner feed you 20 medium-speed topspin returns from his backhand side to your backhand side. Alternate between returning the ball with a backhand counterdrive (first gear) and returning it with a topspin block.

To Increase Difficulty

- Have your practice partner turn and use his forehand topspin from his backhand side to feed the balls.

Success Check

- Contact the ball as it rises.
- Contact the ball above the center of the ball's face.
- Keep the stroke short, using the wrist to impart added topspin.

Score Your Success

17 to 20 successful blocks = 10 points

13 to 16 successful blocks = 5 points

9 to 12 successful blocks = 1 point

Your score ___

Intermediate Strokes Drill 2. *Alternating Backhand Counterdrives and Punch Block Returns*

Have your practice partner feed you 20 medium-speed topspin returns from her backhand side to your backhand side. Alternate between returning the ball with a backhand counterdrive (first gear) and returning it with a punch block. If your practice partner has problems returning your punch blocks, she can feed balls using the multiball method.

To Increase Difficulty

- Have your practice partner turn and use her forehand topspin from her backhand side to feed the balls.

Success Check

- Contact the ball as it rises.
- Contact the ball above the center of the ball's face.
- Keep the stroke short and snap the wrist forward and down at contact to impart speed to the return.
- Make force contact.

Score Your Success

17 to 20 successful blocks = 10 points

13 to 16 successful blocks = 5 points

9 to 12 successful blocks = 1 point

Your score ___

Intermediate Strokes Drill 3. *Alternating Backhand Counterdrives and Sidespin Block Returns*

Have your practice partner feed you 20 strong topspin returns from his backhand side to your backhand side. Alternate between returning the ball with a backhand counterdrive (first gear) and returning it with a sidespin block. You may use either right or left sidespin. If your practice partner has problems returning your sidespin blocks, he can feed balls using the multiball method.

To Increase Difficulty

- Have your practice partner turn and use his forehand topspin from his backhand side to feed the balls.

Success Check

- Contact the ball as it rises.
- Contact the ball above the center of the ball's face on the right side (right sidespin) or left side (left sidespin).
- Keep the stroke short.
- Finish with the racket on the right side of the body (right sidespin block) or on the left side of the body (left sidespin block).

Score Your Success

17 to 20 successful blocks = 10 points

13 to 16 successful blocks = 5 points

9 to 12 successful blocks = 1 point

Your score ___

Intermediate Strokes Drill 4. *Alternating Backhand Counterdrives and Chop Block Returns*

Have your practice partner feed you 20 medium-speed topspin returns from his backhand side to your backhand side. Alternate between returning the ball with a backhand counterdrive (first gear) and returning it with a chop block. If your practice partner has problems returning your chop blocks, he can feed balls using the multiball method.

To Increase Difficulty

- Have your practice partner turn and use his forehand topspin from his backhand side to feed the balls.

Success Check

- Contact the ball as it rises.
- Contact the ball above the center of the ball's face with a closed racket that is moving down, not forward.
- Keep the stroke short.
- Snap the wrist down at contact, brushing the ball to produce backspin.

Score Your Success

17 to 20 successful blocks = 10 points

13 to 16 successful blocks = 5 points

9 to 12 successful blocks = 1 point

Your score ___

ADDING SIDESPIN TO TOPSPIN STROKES

Intermediate players often add some sidespin to topspin strokes to create wider angles for their opponents to cover. To produce these topspin–sidespin returns, your racket must strike the ball more toward the outside or inside edge while still moving upward to produce topspin. This means that your racket does not travel straight through the ball. Instead, it travels around the edge of the ball. Because this stroke can lead to more errors, use it only as a variation and not as your primary topspin stroke. Although you can add either left or right sidespin to a topspin stroke, right sidespin is used most often and is easier for a right-handed player to learn. Using left sidespin with a topspin return requires major modifications in strokes and is not as popular for that reason.

Forehand Topspin With Sidespin

A right-handed player commonly uses this stroke when he is forced wide to his forehand and usually directs the stroke toward the opponent's wide forehand. The sidespin causes the ball to break very wide and pulls the opponent off the table.

When executed by a left-handed player, this stroke carries left sidespin and both curves to the right and breaks sharply to the right after hitting the table.

Three Basic Elements for the Forehand Topspin With Sidespin

How to touch the ball = friction contact

When to touch the ball = at the top of the bounce or as the ball is descending

Where to touch the ball = against topspin, on the right side of the ball and above the center; against backspin, on the right side of the ball and below the center

Begin the forehand topspin with sidespin stroke as you would a normal forehand topspin stroke. However, during the backswing phase, position the racket more behind your back instead of bringing it straight back. This will allow you to swing your racket toward your right across the ball (if you are a right-handed player) to contact the right edge of the ball, the side of the ball farthest away from you. You will produce some right sidespin along with your normal topspin. This will cause the ball to curve to your left during flight and break sharply to the left after striking the table.

Misstep

Your strokes lack sidespin.

Correction

Make sure your racket contacts the side of the ball.

Misstep

The ball sails long on your returns.

Correction

Focus on brushing upward on the ball to produce topspin. You want to add only a small amount of sidespin by contacting the side of the ball. If you add too much sidespin, you will lose the topspin necessary for bringing the ball down on the table.

Backhand Topspin With Sidespin

For right-handed players, this stroke often is used to direct the ball down the line without needing to move the feet out of the normal ready position with the left foot forward. Because your body will be in the way of your swing, you will not be able to produce as much sidespin as you can on the forehand side.

When executed by a left-handed player (figure 9.7), this stroke carries left sidespin and both curves to the right and breaks to the right after hitting the table.

Three Basic Elements for the Backhand Topspin With Sidespin

How to touch the ball = friction contact

When to touch the ball = at the top of the bounce for maximum power or as the ball is descending for maximum spin

Where to touch the ball = against topspin, on the right side of the ball and above the center of the face of the ball; against backspin, on the right side of the ball and below the center of the face of the ball.

The backhand topspin with sidespin stroke is similar to the normal backhand topspin. The main exception is that during the backswing phase, you bring the racket back to the left side of your hip. This allows you to swing your racket more toward your right across the ball (if you are right-handed) to contact the right edge of the ball while still moving the racket upward to produce topspin. To accomplish this, your wrist will have to turn inward, toward you, at contact. This will cause the ball to curve to your left during flight and break to your left after striking the table.

Figure 9.7	Backhand Topspin With Sidespin, Left–Handed Player

BACKSWING

1. Transfer weight to right leg by bending right knee
2. Bring racket off side of right hip
3. Racket is in closed position
4. Wrist laid back

a

(continued)

Figure 9.7 *(continued)*

CONTACT

1. Transfer weight from right to left foot
2. Move racket forward, up, and to left
3. Contact ball in center of backhand triangle
4. Racket is in closed position
5. Racket contacts ball above center of ball's face and on left side
6. Racket swings from right to left
7. Forearm and wrist snap to produce maximum racket acceleration

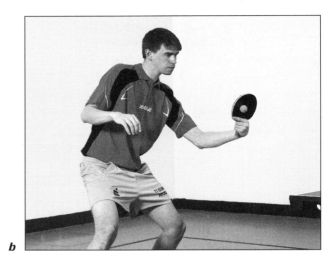

b

FOLLOW-THROUGH

1. Arm continues to rotate around elbow to finish about shoulder height and on left side of body
2. Wrist in forward position at finish
3. Racket finishes in closed position
4. Relax racket hand and return to ready position

c

Misstep

You have problems returning your opponent's topspin–sidespin returns.

Correction

A topspin–sidespin return will jump sideways when it hits your side of the table. To return this stroke, do not aim where the ball will contact the table, but anticipate the curve. Aim for where the ball will be when you contact it.

Intermediate Strokes Drill 5. *Forehand Topspins With Right Sidespin Against Topspin Returns*

Have your practice partner feed 30 steady topspin drives crosscourt to your forehand side. Return the first two with your normal forehand topspin. On your third return, add some right sidespin. If you execute the stroke correctly (and are right-handed), the ball should break sharply to your left when it hits the table. Repeat the pattern until you have attempted to add right sidespin to your topspin return 10 times.

To Increase Difficulty

- Have the feeder increase the amount of spin on the returns.
- Have the feeder increase the speed of the returns.

To Decrease Difficulty

- Have the feeder decrease the amount of spin on the returns.
- Have the feeder decrease the speed of the returns.

Success Check

- Make sure your backswing position for the forehand topspin with right sidespin is behind your back.
- Ask your practice partner for feedback on the amount of sidespin you are generating with your stroke.

Score Your Success

9 or 10 successful topspin with right sidespin returns = 10 points

7 or 8 successful topspin with right sidespin returns = 5 points

5 or 6 successful topspin with right sidespin returns = 1 point

Your score ____

Intermediate Strokes Drill 6. *Forehand Topspins With Right Sidespin Against Backspin Returns*

Have your practice partner use the multiball method to feed 30 backspin balls to your forehand. Return the first two balls with forehand topspins; then on the third ball, execute a forehand topspin with right sidespin. If done correctly, the ball should break sharply to your left after contacting the table. Repeat the pattern until you have attempted to add right sidespin to your topspin return 10 times.

To Increase Difficulty

- Have the feeder increase the amount of backspin on the ball feeds.

To Decrease Difficulty

- Have the feeder decrease the amount of backspin on the ball feeds.

Success Check

- Contact the ball as it descends to create maximum spin.
- When adding right sidespin, bring your backswing more behind your back to allow you to swing across the ball.
- Make sure the racket contacts the ball below the center of the ball's face and on the right side of the ball.

Score Your Success

9 or 10 successful topspin with right sidespin returns = 10 points

7 or 8 successful topspin with right sidespin returns = 5 points

5 or 6 successful topspin with right sidespin returns = 1 point

Your score ___

Intermediate Strokes Drill 7. Backhand Topspins With Right Sidespin Against Topspin Returns

Have your practice partner use the multiball method to feed 30 medium-speed topspin balls to your backhand side. Execute two backhand topspins crosscourt and then, by adding right sidespin to your backhand topspin, direct your third return down the line. If done properly, you will be able to direct the ball down the line without moving your feet out of the normal ready position with the left foot forward. Repeat the pattern until you have attempted to add right sidespin to your backhand topspin return 10 times.

To Increase Difficulty

- Have the feeder increase the amount of spin on the ball feeds.
- Have the feeder increase the speed of the ball feeds.

To Decrease Difficulty

- Have the feeder decrease the amount of spin on the ball feeds.
- Have the feeder decrease the speed of the ball feeds.

Success Check

- When you add right sidespin, your backswing position is more to the left side of your body.
- When you add right sidespin, the ball should break to the left after contacting the table.
- The racket should contact the ball above the center of the ball's face and on the right side of the ball.
- Ask your practice partner for feedback on the amount of right sidespin you are generating.

Score Your Success

9 or 10 successful backhand topspin with right sidespin returns = 10 points

7 or 8 successful backhand topspin with right sidespin returns = 5 points

5 or 6 successful backhand topspin with right sidespin returns = 1 point

Your score ___

Intermediate Strokes Drill 8. *Backhand Topspins With Right Sidespin Against Backspin Returns*

Have your practice partner use the multiball method to feed 30 backspin returns to your backhand. Return the first two balls crosscourt using backhand topspins. Return the third ball down the line with a backhand topspin with right sidespin. Repeat the pattern until you have attempted to add right sidespin to your backhand topspin return 10 times.

To Increase Difficulty

- Have the feeder increase the amount of backspin on the ball feeds.

To Decrease Difficulty

- Have the feeder decrease the amount of backspin on the ball feeds.

Success Check

- Contact the ball as it descends to produce maximum spin.
- When you add right sidespin, your backswing should be more to the left side of your body.
- When you add right sidespin, the ball should break to the left when it contacts the table.
- Ask your practice partner for feedback on the amount of sidespin you are generating.

Score Your Success

9 or 10 successful backhand topspin with right sidespin returns = 10 points

7 or 8 successful backhand topspin with right sidespin returns = 5 points

5 or 6 successful backhand topspin with right sidespin returns = 1 point

Your score ___

PLAYING DEFENSIVE STROKES

Defensive strokes are played from a deep position, away from the table. Chopping players use chop strokes to try to force the opponent to commit outright errors or weak returns that they can attack to finish the point. When you execute a chop return against topspin, you are going with (adding to) the spin, so it is possible to produce very high spin returns. To be effective, chop returns must land low and deep on the opponent's side of the table.

Three Basic Elements for the Chop Stroke

How to touch the ball = with maximum friction

When to touch the ball = as the ball is descending

Where to touch the ball = toward the bottom of the ball's face

When forced into a defensive position, offensive players normally use high topspin returns, or lobs, to try to gain time to get back into position to counterattack. To be effective, lob returns need to carry a lot of topspin and land deep on the table. The idea is to push the attacker back off the table and create an opening to counterattack. Topspin attackers may also use occasional chop strokes when in a defensive position.

Three Basic Elements for the Lob

How to touch the ball = with maximum friction

When to touch the ball = as the ball is descending

Where to touch the ball = above the center of the ball

Backhand Chop Against Topspin

For the backhand chop against topspin (figure 9.8), from a neutral ready position, bring your left leg back and rotate your shoulders and hips to your left so that your body is sideways, facing to your left (right-handed player). As your left leg moves back, bend your elbow and cock your wrist upward so that the racket is at about shoulder height and pointing upward. The forearm moves down and forward to allow the racket to contact the ball as it is descending. Make contact toward the bottom of the ball. At contact with the ball, snap your wrist to increase racket acceleration to produce a heavy backspin return. Follow through toward your target, returning your body and racket to the ready position. From the beginning through the recovery, the stroke has a circular feel.

With practice, you will learn to vary the amount of wrist you use and also the contact point to change the amount of backspin you produce.

| Figure 9.8 | **Backhand Chop** |

BACKSWING

1. Step back with left leg into wide stance
2. Rotate shoulders and hips to left
3. Transfer weight to back foot
4. Bring racket to shoulder height
5. Racket points up
6. Elbow bent

a

b

c

CONTACT

1. Begin to transfer weight from back foot to front foot
2. Move forearm down and forward to contact bottom part of ball
3. Snap wrist at contact to add racket acceleration and increase amount of backspin

FOLLOW-THROUGH

1. Racket continues toward target
2. Wrist has fully snapped from high to low
3. Recover to ready position

Misstep

Your chop returns lack spin.

Correction

Make sure your wrist is cocked upward at the beginning of the stroke and snaps downward at contact.

Misstep

You find it difficult to chop balls that are still rising when chopping from mid-distance.

Correction

Start your backswing higher, around head height, and swing downward more.

Forehand Chop Against Topspin

For the forehand chop against topspin (figure 9.9), from a neutral ready position, step back with your right leg and rotate your upper body and hips to the right (right-handed player). At the same time, bend your elbow and cock your wrist upward so that the racket is at about shoulder height and pointing up.

The mechanics of the forehand chop are the same as those of the backhand chop. The forearm moves down and forward to allow the racket to contact the ball as it descends. Make contact toward the bottom of the ball. At contact with the ball, snap your wrist downward to increase racket acceleration to produce a heavy backspin return. Follow through toward your target, returning your body and racket to the ready position. From the beginning through the recovery, the stroke has a circular feel.

Figure 9.9   **Forehand Chop**

BACKSWING

1. Step back with right leg into wide stance
2. Rotate shoulders and hips to right
3. Transfer weight to back foot
4. Bring racket to shoulder height
5. Racket points up
6. Elbow bent

a

CONTACT

1. Begin to transfer weight from back foot to front foot
2. Move forearm down and forward to contact bottom part of ball
3. Snap wrist at contact to add racket acceleration and increase amount of backspin

b

FOLLOW-THROUGH

1. Racket continues toward target
2. Wrist has fully snapped from high to low
3. Recover to ready position

c

Misstep

Returns go long against heavy topspins.

Correction

Chop downward more at contact.

Misstep

Returns go into the net.

Correction

Follow through more forward toward your target.

Forehand Lob Against Fast Topspin or Smash

Play the forehand lob stroke (figure 9.10) from a deep position, away from the table. Begin in the forehand topspin stance with the foot on your nonracket side forward. Rotate your body to the right (if right-handed) or left (if left-handed) with the shoulder on your racket side lower than your other shoulder. Your elbow is open and the racket is at around knee height. Move your forearm upward to allow the racket to contact the ball at about waist height. The swing is mostly upward, with the racket brushing the ball to produce topspin. The racket finishes at about head height. To be effective, the lob return must land deep on the opponent's side of the table and have heavy topspin to cause it to jump forward on contact. You can also add sidespin to move your opponent off the table.

Figure 9.10 Forehand Lob

BACKSWING

1. Deep position from table
2. Forehand topspin stance
3. Weight on back foot
4. Rotate upper body so shoulder on racket side is lower
5. Racket is at about knee height and points down

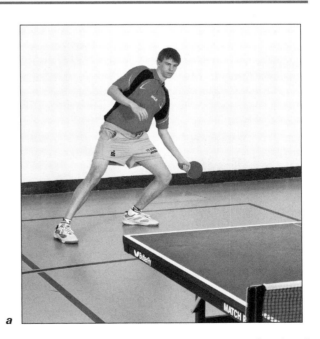

a

(continued)

Figure 9.10 *(continued)*

b

c

CONTACT

1. Begin to transfer weight to front foot
2. Rotate shoulders
3. Bring racket up to contact ball at about waist height
4. Racket contacts ball above center of ball's face, making friction contact to create topspin
5. At contact, forearm and wrist snap up and forward to add to spin

FOLLOW-THROUGH

1. Weight fully transferred to front foot
2. Racket finishes at about head height and pointing up

Misstep

Returns lack topspin.

Correction

Make sure to contact the ball as it is descending and kick up your wrist at contact.

Backhand Lob Against Fast Topspin or Smash

The backhand lob stroke (figure 9.11) is also played from a deep position, away from the table. Begin in a sideways stance with the foot on your nonracket side back. Rotate your body to the left (if right-handed) or right (if left-handed) with your racket-side shoulder lower than your other shoulder. Your elbow is open and the racket is at about knee height. Move your forearm upward to allow the racket to contact the ball at about waist height. The swing is mostly upward, with the racket brushing the ball to produce topspin. The racket finishes at about head height. Once again, to produce an effective return, the lob must land deep on the opponent's side of the table and carry heavy topspin. You can also add sidespin to move your opponent off the table.

Figure 9.11 Backhand Lob

BACKSWING

1. Deep position from table
2. Backhand topspin stance with racket-side foot forward
3. Weight on back foot
4. Rotate upper body, racket-side shoulder lower
5. Racket is at about knee height and points down

a

CONTACT

1. Begin to transfer weight to front foot
2. Rotate shoulders
3. Bring racket up to contact ball at about waist height
4. Racket contacts ball above center of ball's face, making friction contact to create topspin
5. At contact, forearm and wrist snap up

b

FOLLOW-THROUGH

1. Weight has fully transferred to front foot
2. Racket finishes at about head height and points up

c

Misstep

You lack control of your returns.

Correction

Make sure to get your body sideways to the ball so you can use a full stroke.

Intermediate Strokes Drill 9. *Backhand Chops Against Topspin*

Have your practice partner feed you 20 topspin balls to your backhand using the multiball technique described in step 1 (page 9). From mid-distance from the table, return all balls using a backhand chop. Try to place the first 10 returns crosscourt and then the next 10 down the line.

To Increase Difficulty

- Have the feeder increase the amount of spin on the ball feeds.
- Have the feeder increase the speed of the ball feeds.

To Decrease Difficulty

- Have the feeder decrease the amount of spin on the ball feeds.
- Have the feeder decrease the speed of the ball feeds.

Success Check

- Make sure your wrist and racket point up in the backswing position.
- Contact the bottom of the ball as it descends.
- Follow through toward your target.
- Recover to a neutral ready position.

Score Your Success

17 to 20 successful backhand chops = 10 points

13 to 16 successful backhand chops = 5 points

9 to 12 successful backhand chops = 1 point

Your score ___

Intermediate Strokes Drill 10. *Forehand Chops Against Topspin*

Have your practice partner feed 20 topspin balls to your forehand using the multiball technique described in step 1 (page 9). From mid-distance from the table, return all balls using a forehand chop. Try to place the first 10 returns crosscourt and then the next 10 down the line.

To Increase Difficulty

- Have the feeder increase the amount of spin on the ball feeds.
- Have the feeder increase the speed of the ball feeds.

To Decrease Difficulty

- Have the feeder decrease the amount of spin on the ball feeds.
- Have the feeder decrease the speed of the ball feeds.

Success Check

- Make sure your wrist and racket point up in the backswing position.
- Contact the bottom of the ball as it descends.
- Follow through toward your target.
- Recover to a neutral ready position.

Score Your Success

17 to 20 successful forehand chops = 10 points

13 to 16 successful forehand chops = 5 points

9 to 12 successful forehand chops = 1 point

Your score ___

Intermediate Strokes Drill 11. *Mixed Backhand and Forehand Chops Against Topspin*

Have your practice partner use the multiball method to feed you 20 strong topspin balls. He should alternate between sending one ball to your backhand side and one to your forehand side. Return the first with a backhand chop and the second with a forehand chop and then continue to alternate. Return all balls crosscourt.

To Increase Difficulty

- Have the feeder increase the amount of spin on the ball feeds.
- Have the feeder increase the speed of the ball feeds.

To Decrease Difficulty

- Have the feeder decrease the amount of spin on the ball feeds.
- Have the feeder decrease the speed of the ball feeds.

Success Check

- Make sure your wrist and racket point up in the backswing position for both backhand and forehand chops.
- Contact the bottom of the ball as it descends.
- Follow through toward your target.
- Recover to a neutral ready position between strokes.

Score Your Success

17 to 20 successful chops = 10 points

13 to 16 successful chops = 5 points

9 to 12 successful chops = 1 point

Your score ___

Intermediate Strokes Drill 12. *Forehand Lob With Ball Drop*

You can do this drill by yourself. From a deep position, drop a ball with your free hand from about shoulder height. Using a forehand lob stroke, send the ball high and deep onto the other side of the table, generating as much topspin as possible. Watch your return to see how deeply it lands and how much the ball kicks off the table. Hit 10 forehand lobs.

To Increase Difficulty

- Add some sidespin to your returns.

Success Check

- Start the stroke with your body in a forehand topspin position with the racket at knee height.
- Your right shoulder should be lower than your left.
- At contact, brush up with your forearm and wrist to impart maximum topspin.
- Your lobs should travel high over the net and land deep on the other side of the table.

Score Your Success

9 or 10 successful forehand lobs = 10 points

7 or 8 successful forehand lobs = 5 points

5 or 6 successful forehand lobs = 1 point

Your score ___

Intermediate Strokes Drill 13. *Forehand Lob Against Smash*

Have your practice partner use a forehand to smash 10 balls to your forehand. Using a forehand lob stroke, return all balls high and deep to your partner's forehand. Try to add as much topspin as possible to your returns.

To Increase Difficulty

- Have the feeder add more speed to the smashes.

To Decrease Difficulty

- Have the feeder use the multiball method to feed balls.

Success Check

- Move your body to the ball while in the forehand topspin position.

- Your right shoulder should be lower than your left.
- Try to contact the ball as it is falling and when it is at about waist height.
- Snap your forearm and wrist up at contact to produce maximum topspin.
- Follow through to head height.
- Recover to a neutral ready position between strokes.

Score Your Success

9 or 10 successful forehand lobs = 10 points

7 or 8 successful forehand lobs = 5 points

5 or 6 successful forehand lobs = 1 point

Your score ___

Intermediate Strokes Drill 14. *Backhand Lob With Ball Drop*

You can do this drill by yourself. From a deep position, drop a ball with your free hand from about shoulder height. Using a backhand lob stroke, send the ball high and deep onto the other side of the table, generating as much topspin as possible. Watch your return to see how deeply it lands and how much the ball kicks off the table. Hit 10 backhand lobs.

To Increase Difficulty

- Add some sidespin to your returns.

Success Check

- Start the stroke with your body in a backhand topspin position and the racket at knee height.

- Your right shoulder should be lower than your left.
- At contact, brush up with your forearm and wrist to impart maximum topspin.
- Your lobs should travel high over the net and land deep on the other side of the table.

Score Your Success

9 or 10 successful backhand lobs = 10 points

7 or 8 successful backhand lobs = 5 points

5 or 6 successful backhand lobs = 1 point

Your score ___

Intermediate Strokes Drill 15. *Backhand Lob Against Smash*

Have your practice partner use a forehand to smash 10 balls to your backhand side. Using a backhand lob stroke, return all balls high and deep to your partner's forehand. Try to add as much topspin as possible to your returns.

To Increase Difficulty

- Have the feeder add more speed to the smashes.

To Decrease Difficulty

- Have the feeder use the multiball method to feed balls.

Success Check

- Move your body to the ball while in the backhand topspin position.

- Your right shoulder should be lower than your left.
- Try to contact the ball as it is falling and when it is at about waist height.
- Snap your forearm and wrist up at contact to produce maximum topspin.
- Follow through to head height.
- Recover to a neutral ready position between strokes.

Score Your Success

9 or 10 successful backhand lobs = 10 points

7 or 8 successful backhand lobs = 5 points

5 or 6 successful backhand lobs = 1 point

Your score ___

USING THE FOREHAND SMASH, OR KILL

Every player needs to be able to execute a point-winning forehand smash against a high return, especially once the ball has bounced higher than shoulder height. Balls this high are very difficult to apply topspin to. Although power loopers and attacking choppers most often rely on fast forehand topspins as their point-winning strokes, counterdrivers, close-to-the-table defenders, and all-around attackers use the smash more often.

Although the mechanics of the drive and the smash are basically the same, the smash requires a longer follow-through and a complete weight shift from the back foot to the front foot.

Three Basic Elements for the Forehand Smash

How to touch the ball = maximum force contact; against topspin, force is directed forward and down; against backspin, force is directed forward and up

When to touch the ball = at the top of the bounce

Where to touch the ball = against backspin, below the center of the ball's face; against topspin, above the center of the ball's face

To increase the speed of the smash, you must increase the acceleration of your racket while the ball is on the racket. Because the ball stays on the racket for only a short time, this racket acceleration is very explosive. Many studies have shown that elite players have slower swings into the ball, but great acceleration on contact with the ball.

Power comes from the lower body. It is transferred to and out the playing arm and is applied to the ball by the racket at contact. The key to this process is the explosive transfer of body weight from your back foot to your front foot. To load the weight on your back foot, rotate your upper body back into the forehand backswing position and bend your right knee as all your body weight falls onto your back foot (figure

9.12*a*). The forward swing occurs in reverse order, with the right leg pushing hard off the ground and the hips and upper body rotating to the left (figure 9.12*b*). At contact, the forehand snaps, transferring all of the stored energy of the body into the ball (figure 9.12*c*).

Figure 9.12 Forehand Smash Against Backspin Return

BACKSWING

1. Move to ball
2. Rotate upper body and hips to right
3. Deeply bend right knee to shift all body weight to right foot
4. Extend playing arm so it points back and is lower than oncoming ball

a

CONTACT AGAINST BACKSPIN

1. Push hard off right foot
2. Rotate hips and upper body to left
3. At contact, forearm begins to snap, releasing power generated by lower body onto ball
4. Make contact at top of bounce for maximum speed
5. Racket is open
6. Contact ball below center of ball's face

b

FOLLOW-THROUGH

1. Hips and shoulders have completely rotated to left
2. Racket finishes head high and on left side of body
3. Arm is bent at elbow, indicating that forearm snap occurred
4. Right foot falls forward to help maintain balance
5. To recover to ready position, push back off right foot

c

Misstep

When smashing against a backspin ball, your returns hit the net.

Correction

Open your racket face more so that you contact the ball farther below the ball's center. Push up more on contact.

Laboratory studies have shown that the weight transfer happens so quickly that when the racket contacts the ball, the player's weight is actually off the ground or barely skimming along the surface (figure 9.13). This is referred to as being *unweighted* (no body weight pushing down on the ground). Because the hips are rotating so quickly, at the end of the stroke the right foot falls forward to maintain balance. To recover to the ready position, push back off the right foot.

A smash can be executed against either a backspin or topspin return. Although the smash stroke is basically the same against both spins, the point of contact with the ball and the direction of force when the racket contacts the ball differ. Whenever you apply force (forward speed) to the ball, you apply the force in two directions.

Figure 9.13 At contact, the feet skim along the ground. This is known as being unweighted.

Against topspin, the direction of force is forward and down. Against backspin, the direction of force is forward and up (figure 9.14).

| **Figure 9.14** | **Contact for Forehand Smash Against Topspin Return** |

CONTACT AGAINST TOPSPIN

1. Push hard off right foot
2. Rotate hips and upper body to left
3. At contact, forearm begins to snap, releasing power generated by lower body onto ball
4. Make contact at top of bounce for maximum speed
5. Racket is closed
6. Contact ball above center of ball's face
7. Feet barely touch floor (unweighted)

Misstep

When smashing against a topspin ball, your returns go long and do not hit your opponent's side of the table.

Correction

Close your racket face more so that you contact the ball farther above the ball's center. Press down more at contact.

Note that any ball, regardless of its height or amount of spin, can be smashed. However, the smash can be executed only at the top of the bounce. Because the smash travels very low over the net, it is a lower-percentage stroke compared to a fast topspin return. For this reason, many players use a smash only against a high, bouncing return.

Intermediate Strokes Drill 16. *Forehand Smash Against Backspin*

For this drill, ask your practice partner to use the multiball method to feed three long backspin balls to your forehand side. Use a forehand topspin to return the first two balls; then smash the third ball. Direct the smash crosscourt. Repeat this pattern 10 times for a total of 30 balls.

To Increase Difficulty

- Have the feeder increase the amount of backspin and lower the height of the balls she feeds.

To Decrease Difficulty

- Have the feeder reduce the amount of backspin and feed balls so they bounce higher.

Success Check

- Transfer your body weight from your back foot to your front foot at the moment you contact the ball.

- At contact with the ball, you should feel unweighted.
- Contact the ball below the center of the ball's face and push forward and up.
- Make sure your right foot falls forward as you follow through.

Score Your Success

9 or 10 successful forehand smashes = 10 points

7 or 8 successful forehand smashes = 5 points

5 or 6 successful forehand smashes = 1 point

Your score ___

Intermediate Strokes Drill 17. *Forehand Smash Against Topspin*

Ask your practice partner to use the multiball feeding method to send two topspin balls to your backhand and then one to your forehand. Use a backhand counterdrive to return the first two balls crosscourt; then smash the third ball crosscourt with your forehand. Repeat the pattern 10 times for a total of 30 balls.

To Increase Difficulty

- Have the feeder increase the amount of topspin and lower the height of the balls he feeds.

To Decrease Difficulty

- Have the feeder reduce the amount of topspin and feed balls so they bounce higher.

Success Check

- Transfer your body weight from your back foot to your front foot at the moment you contact the ball.
- At contact with the ball, you should feel unweighted.

- Contact the ball above the center of the ball's face and push forward and down.
- Make sure your right foot falls forward as you follow through.

Score Your Success

9 or 10 successful forehand smashes = 10 points

7 or 8 successful forehand smashes = 5 points

5 or 6 successful forehand smashes = 1 point

Your score ___

Intermediate Strokes Drill 18. *Falkenberg Drill With Two Forehand Smashes*

This is a variation of the Falkenberg drill introduced in step 3. For this drill, ask your practice partner to feed two topspin balls to your backhand side and then one to your forehand side. Return the first ball with a backhand counterdrive; then pivot into the backhand corner and execute a forehand smash on the second ball. Then push back into the ready position and move to your forehand side to make a second forehand smash against the third ball. Repeat the pattern 10 times for a total of 30 balls.

To Increase Difficulty

- Have the feeder increase the frequency of the ball feeds.
- Have the feeder mix topspin and backhand feeds.

To Decrease Difficulty

- Have the feeder decrease the speed of the ball feeds.

Success Check

- Transfer your body weight from your back foot to your front foot at the moment you contact the ball.
- At contact with the ball, you should feel unweighted.
- Contact the ball above the center of the ball's face and push forward and down.
- Make sure your right foot falls forward as you follow through.

Score Your Success

18 to 20 successful forehand smashes = 10 points

15 to 17 successful forehand smashes = 5 points

12 to 14 successful forehand smashes = 1 point

Your score ___

SUCCESS SUMMARY OF PLAYING INTERMEDIATE STROKES

This step introduced a variety of intermediate stroke techniques. You should understand all of these techniques because they will occur in match play. However, you should select which techniques match well with your personal style of play and concentrate on perfecting those. Few players will use all of these techniques.

To see whether you are ready to move on to step 10, add up your drill scores. If you scored at least 150 points, you are ready to move on to step 10. If not, practice more to improve your scores.

Intermediate Strokes Drills

1.	Alternating Backhand Counterdrives and Topspin Block Returns	___ out of 10
2.	Alternating Backhand Counterdrives and Punch Block Returns	___ out of 10
3.	Alternating Backhand Counterdrives and Sidespin Block Returns	___ out of 10
4.	Alternating Backhand Counterdrives and Chop Block Returns	___ out of 10
5.	Forehand Topspins With Right Sidespin Against Topspin Returns	___ out of 10
6.	Forehand Topspins With Right Sidespin Against Backspin Returns	___ out of 10
7.	Backhand Topspins With Right Sidespin Against Topspin Returns	___ out of 10
8.	Backhand Topspins With Right Sidespin Against Backspin Returns	___ out of 10
9.	Backhand Chops Against Topspin	___ out of 10
10.	Forehand Chops Against Topspin	___ out of 10
11.	Mixed Backhand and Forehand Chops Against Topspin	___ out of 10
12.	Forehand Lob With Ball Drop	___ out of 10
13.	Forehand Lob Against Smash	___ out of 10
14.	Backhand Lob With Ball Drop	___ out of 10
15.	Backhand Lob Against Smash	___ out of 10
16.	Forehand Smash Against Backspin	___ out of 10
17.	Forehand Smash Against Topspin	___ out of 10
18.	Falkenberg Drill With Two Forehand Smashes	___ out of 10
Total		___ *out of 180*

The next step in your development path will be to revisit the two most important strokes in the game, the serve and the serve return. Step 10 introduces the advanced serve and serve return techniques that you will need to prepare for tournament play.

Performing Intermediate Serves

In step 5, you learned to perform a variety of basic serves. In this step, you will learn to add the critical element of deception to your serves. The drills in this step will give you the opportu- nity not only to practice your serves but also to practice using serves effectively in match play against various styles of play.

ADDING DECEPTION TO SERVES

No matter how good your serve is, if your op- ponent can read the type and amount of spin on it, he will be able to make an effective return. For this reason, you must learn to disguise both the type and amount of spin on your serves. The better your opponents are, the greater your need to develop deceptive serves will be.

Recent rule changes prevent the server from using his free arm to hide the contact of the racket with the ball. This makes disguising the spin on the ball more difficult for the server. However, there are still ways to make it difficult for your opponent to read your serve.

Changing the Amount of Spin

The most obvious way to change the amount of spin on a serve is to change the amount of racket acceleration when you contact the ball. However, this tactic will be visible to your opponent. The deceptive way to change spin is to make contact with various parts of your racket.

During the serve, the end of the racket (A) moves faster than the handle (B) (figure 10.1). A

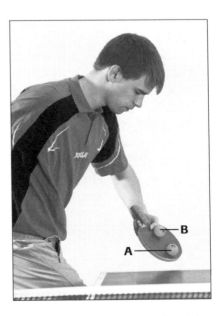

Figure 10.1 Racket in serve position, head down. The end of the racket (A) moves faster than the handle (B) during the serve.

179

ball struck toward the end of the racket (A) will have more spin than one struck toward the handle (B). By changing where on the racket you hit the ball, you can change the amount of spin on your serve while keeping constant racket speed from serve to serve, making reading the amount of spin very difficult for your opponent.

Misstep

You have difficulty producing no-spin serves.

Correction

Make sure the ball contacts your racket toward the handle and not toward the end of the blade.

Disguising the Type of Spin

The receiver will try to read the type of spin on your serve by closely watching where your racket contacts the ball. The double-motion serve disguises the point of contact. It is commonly used by many tournament level players.

The double-motion serve is also called the *pendulum serve* because the movement of the arm swinging from the elbow resembles the back-and-forth motion of a pendulum. To produce this serve, the server appears to swing twice at the ball very quickly with the racket first moving toward the body and then away from the body. The ball can be contacted with the racket moving in either direction; the other motion serves as a fake.

Although the double-motion principle can be applied to any serve, it is most often used with the forehand serve. To execute a forehand double-motion serve (figure 10.2), take a position completely off to the nonracket side of the table, so that your nonracket hand is at the side line. (A right-handed player would stand off to the left side of the table; a left-handed player, as shown in figure 10.2, would stand off the right side of the table.) Use the serve grip. The foot on your nonracket side should be in front of your other foot, and your upper body should be parallel to the side line of the table. Your racket hand and your free hand, which is holding the ball, are close together at the start of the serve.

From an open palm, toss the ball at least 6 inches (15 cm) high. At the same time, rotate your upper body to bring your racket back to the ready position. Immediately after the toss, remove your free hand from the area between your body and the table so that the ball is visible to your opponent throughout the serve.

As the ball begins to descend, rotate back toward the ball and bring the racket to the ball. Snap your wrist toward your body and then quickly away from your body. This allows you to contact the ball as your wrist moves toward your body (left sidespin for a right-handed player, right sidespin for a left-handed player) or as your wrist moves away from your body (right sidespin for a right-handed player, left sidespin for a left-handed player; figure 10.3). Use mostly friction contact because you are trying to produce varying amounts of spin, not speed. An open racket face at contact also will add some backspin to the serve. A closed racket face at contact will add some topspin to the serve. With practice, the whole serve motion (both directions) occurs very quickly, making it difficult for an opponent to see where the actual contact takes place.

Figure 10.2 **Forehand Double-Motion Serve**

BEGINNING POSITION

1. Stand outside side line
2. Foot on nonracket side slightly in front of other foot
3. Upper body parallel to side line
4. Serve grip
5. Hands close together

a

BACKSWING

1. Throw ball up
2. Rotate upper body to racket side
3. Racket in backswing position
4. Transfer weight to back foot

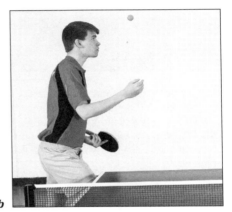

b

CONTACT, RACKET MOVING TOWARD BODY

1. Transfer weight to front foot
2. Rotate upper body, bringing racket to ball
3. Remove free arm from area between body and table so receiver can see ball
4. Pivot forearm around elbow
5. Racket contacts inside edge of ball (part of ball closest to body)
6. Pendulum swing
7. Snap forearm and wrist toward body at contact to produce maximum racket acceleration

c

FOLLOW-THROUGH

1. Snap wrist away from body to disguise point of contact

d

Figure 10.3 Contact with racket moving away from the body during the forehand double-motion serve, left-handed player. The forearm pivots around the elbow, and the racket snaps away from the body in a fake motion. Contact is made on the outside edge of the ball, the part of the ball away from the body.

Using the High-Toss Serve

Another way to add more spin and speed to your serve and at the same time make it more difficult for your opponent to read is to use the high-toss serve. This serve gets its name from the much-higher-than-normal ball toss used to perform the serve. By tossing the ball well overhead, you can use the greater ball speed generated as the ball descends to add more speed and spin to the serve. The receiver often finds it more difficult to visually follow the longer path of the ball, which

adds a deceptive element to the serve. Although this serve can be very effective, it requires a lot of practice to control the toss, which by rule must be nearly vertically straight up.

To execute a high-toss forehand left sidespin serve (figure 10.4), take a position completely off to the left side of the table so that your left hand is at the left side line (right-handed players). Use the serve grip. Your left foot should be in front of your right foot, and your upper body should be parallel to the side line of the table. Your racket hand and your free hand, which is holding the ball, are close together at the start of the serve.

From an open palm, toss the ball 1 to 3 feet (around 30 to 90 cm) above head height as your upper body rotates to the right. Your free hand will have to move up about 6 inches (15 cm) to propel the ball up. The racket and your free hand travel up together; then your racket hand circles back and is brought to the ball in a whiplike action. Immediately after the toss, remove your free hand from the area between your body and the table so the ball is visible to your opponent throughout the serve.

As the ball begins to descend, rotate your body back to the left and bring the racket to the ball. Snap your wrist toward your body and then quickly back away from your body. This allows you to contact the ball on the left side (the wrist moves toward the body) or on the right side (the wrist moves away from the body). Use mostly friction contact because you are trying to produce varying amounts of spin, not speed. An open racket face at contact also will add some backspin to the serve. A closed racket face at contact will add some topspin.

Misstep

You have difficulty producing both right and left sidespin when using the double-motion serve.

Correction

Practice both parts of the serve separately; then combine them using the double-motion concept.

Figure 10.4 High-Toss Forehand Left Sidespin Serve

BEGINNING POSITION

1. Stand outside left side line
2. Left foot slightly in front of right foot
3. Upper body parallel to side line
4. Serve grip
5. Hands close together

BACKSWING

1. Throw ball 1 to 3 feet (30 to 90 cm) above head
2. Rotate upper body to right
3. Racket and free arm in high backswing position
4. Transfer weight to back foot

CONTACT

1. Transfer weight to front foot
2. Rotate upper body to left, bringing racket to ball
3. Remove free arm from area between body and table so receiver can see ball
4. Pivot forearm around elbow to allow racket to contact left side of ball
5. Pendulum swing
6. Snap forearm and wrist toward body at contact to produce maximum racket acceleration

(continued)

Figure 10.4 *(continued)*

FOLLOW-THROUGH

1. After contact, snap wrist away from body to disguise point of contact

d

Misstep

You have difficulty controlling the high-toss serve.

Correction

The key to this serve is the toss. Practice tossing the ball so that it comes straight down into your tossing hand. When you can control the toss, you should be able to control the serve.

Deceptive Serves Drill 1. *One Heavy Backspin Serve, One Light Backspin Serve*

The purpose of this drill is to alternate a heavy backspin serve with a light backspin or no-spin serve by contacting the ball with different parts of your racket. Using the short backspin serve technique described in step 5 (page 75), produce a heavy, short backspin serve by contacting the ball toward the end of the racket. Next, using the same motion, produce a light backspin or no-spin serve by contacting the ball toward your thumb. To be effective, both serves should look as much alike as possible in terms of racket speed, ball speed, and the location of the bounces. Hit 40 serves, alternating between a heavy backspin serve and a light backspin or no-spin serve.

To Increase Difficulty

- Place two standard-size sheets of paper on the table as targets. Try to hit the targets with your serves.

Success Check

- Both heavy and light backspin serves should be made with the same stroke.
- Both heavy and light backspin serves should have the same height and speed.

Score Your Success

Have your practice partner or coach evaluate your serves for both their deception and their amount of spin and rate you on a scale of 1 to 10, with 10 points being the highest score.

Your score ___

Deceptive Serves Drill 2. *Forehand Double-Motion Serves*

Using the double-motion serve technique, execute 40 forehand sidespin serves. The first 20 serves should be left sidespin serves; the second 20 should be right sidespin serves. Try to make the wrist snap in both directions as quick as possible to make the serve as deceptive as possible.

To Increase Difficulty

- Place two standard-size sheets of paper on the table as targets. Try to hit the targets with your serves.

Success Check

- The motions you use for both right and left sidespin serves should be the same.
- Both right and left sidespin serves should have the same height and speed.

Score Your Success

Have your practice partner or coach evaluate your serves for both their deception and their amount of spin and rate you on a scale of 1 to 10, with 10 points being the highest score.

Your score ___

Deceptive Serves Drill 3. *High-Toss Serves*

For this drill, use a normal forehand left sidespin serve as described in step 5 (page 80), but add the high toss. First hit 20 high-toss serves so that the ball lands deep and to your opponent's backhand. Then hit 20 high-toss serves so that the ball lands at mid-depth on your opponent's side of the table. If left untouched, the second bounce on your opponent's side should be at around the end line.

To Increase Difficulty

- Place two standard-size sheets of paper on the table as targets. Place one target deep into the backhand corner and one at mid-depth on the backhand side. Try to hit the targets with your serves.

Success Check

- Use identical-looking motions for both the deep and mid-depth serves.

- The deep serve should bounce close to the opponent's end line.
- The mid-depth serve should bounce a second time on the opponent's side of the table close to the end line.

Score Your Success

17 to 20 successful deep high-toss serves = 10 points

13 to 16 successful deep high-toss serves = 5 points

9 to 12 successful deep high-toss serves = 1 point

17 to 20 successful mid-depth high-toss serves = 10 points

13 to 16 successful mid-depth high-toss serves = 5 points

9 to 12 successful mid-depth high-toss serves = 1 point

Your score ___

PRACTICING SERVES EFFICIENTLY

Serve practice should be a regular part of every practice session. It is a good idea to have a large box of balls on hand so you can serve many times before having to stop to pick up the balls. You can practice serving by yourself, or you can ask a partner to return your serves so that you can practice a whole point. The following techniques will help you get the most out of your serve practice.

Learn only a few service motions, but be able to produce many look-alike variations. Practice contacting various parts of the ball to produce a variety of spins while using the same service delivery. For best results, video record your serve motion. Reviewing your serve motion can help you see whether you give away the type of serve you are using.

Practice serving above your level. A key mistake many people make when practicing serves is that they simply practice the same safe serve they've always used and wonder when it will become a higher-level serve. You have to push yourself to create more spin and improve your placement. If you are practicing serves correctly and pushing yourself, you will miss many serves initially. When you go back to using your normal serve, the consistency will be there but at a much higher level.

Practice your serve as part of the attacking sequence. Remember, your attack is only as strong as its weakest link. The serve and third-ball attack totally rely on each other. The threat of a strong third-ball attack makes the serve return more difficult. Thus, the serve becomes even more effective. Have a practice partner return your serves, and try to make strong third-ball attacks.

Learn to love serving. Great servers really enjoy the creativity of developing their own unique styles. If you don't enjoy serving, you will not practice enough.

Speaking of practice, the best time to practice serving is in the middle of a training session. By that time you are warmed up and your hand skills are at their peak, but you are not physically tired. Serve practice requires a lot of mental energy. Don't wait until the end of practice when you are tired to work on your serve.

If you follow these guidelines, just a few minutes of practice during each training session will pay big dividends. Remember, great servers are not born; they practice.

USING SERVES IN MATCH PLAY

Developing the ability to produce high-quality basic serves and control their placement on the table (step 5) was the first step in developing your own serve game. Adding deception to serves was the second step. The final component to learn is how to use serves effectively during match play.

Each time you serve to an opponent, you should have a clear objective in mind regarding the purpose of that serve. Following are some common objectives:

- Stopping an opponent's attack by serving to a location, usually short, that often forces a passive return.
- Trying to force a weak or medium-speed topspin return from an opponent so that

you can counterattack. These are normally mid-depth serves.

- Winning the point outright by deceiving the receiver about the type or amount of spin you are using.

Basic Serve Strategy

Look for your opponent's serve return weaknesses early during the match. If you are playing an opponent you do not know, serve to a variety of locations early in the match. All players have serve return weaknesses; it is your job to find out what your opponent's weaknesses are. Once you find a weakness, direct the majority of your serves to that area.

Keep your opponent guessing about what serve will be coming. There are several ways to keep your opponent off balance using your serves. The first is by changing the spin on your serves while using the same serve motion. Try to find a serve that your opponent has problems returning and then give him serves that look the same but have different degrees of spin. When he catches on to what you are doing, go back and give him the serve that bothers him. The goal is to keep him guessing and uncomfortable with your serves. Another way to keep your opponent guessing is to vary the depth of your serves. By constantly varying short, medium, and long placements, you can make life difficult for your opponent.

Wait for your opponent's adjustments. When you find an effective serve pattern, continue to use it until your opponent makes an adjustment and begins to make stronger returns. When this happens, try changing the location of your serves for a while and then come back to the original pattern later in the game.

Serve Tactics Against Various Playing Styles

Although every opponent is unique, their games generally fall into one of the basic styles of play discussed in step 8.

The *power looper* has excellent footwork and a strong, dynamic forehand topspin attack. Power loopers are known for their strong short games and will run around deep serves to the backhand side to use their forehand loop. Often, their weakness is returning mid-depth serves, serves in which the second bounce falls close to the end line. A power looper who is unsure whether to loop or flip a return often will take a high-risk shot. Once she misses a few returns, a power looper can lose confidence and will be open to your attack. This style of player also is often insecure against deep, fast serves to her wide forehand.

The *counterdriver* has strong forehand and backhand counterdrives, quick reflexes, and a steady style of play. Most often, these players lack a strong loop. When serving to a counter-driver, use deep backspin or backspin mixed with sidespin serves to the wide backhand. Then attack the return hard to his middle. Also, try serving mid-depth serves into his right elbow and attacking wide to either corner.

The *mid-distance aggressive looper* uses both forehand and backhand loops from several feet (around 1 m) behind the table to win the point. Although he can open off either side, he may prefer to open with his backhand because of the shorter length of the stroke. To avoid playing long loop points, which favor this style, serve mostly short balls. Try mixing chop and no-spin serves and, by all means, attack first. An occasional deep serve into the body can also be effective.

The *attacking chopper* can present a real problem. An attacking chopper uses variations of chop on the backhand combined with chops and strong loops on the forehand. Players of this style often have long-pips rubber on the backhand side of their rackets and often flip their rackets to use different sides when returning serves. When serving to this type of player, emphasize deception and placement over spin. Try to keep your serves out of the middle of the table. Serve very short or very deep, using chop or no spin. Pay close attention to which side of the racket the player uses on the return, and try to attack down the line whenever possible with your third-ball attacks. Be careful when using sidespin serves if the opponent uses long pips. Long pips allow spin to pass through, and your sidespin will be returned in an unpredictable manner, making your next attack more difficult.

The *pips-out penholder* bases her style on a strong forehand hitting game and loves to play fast, taking the ball immediately off the bounce. The pen-hold grip allows for maximum use of the wrist, creating a strong short serve–return game. When serving to this style, use mostly mid-depth serves to the backhand, mixed with an occasional long backspin serve to the back-hand. Because this style of player is anxious to step around and use her forehand from her backhand side, an occasional quick, long serve down the line to her forehand is necessary to keep her honest.

The *close-to-the-table defender* bases his style on a strong defensive backhand blocking game with a controlled forehand offense. Players of this style often have either short- or long-pips rubber on the backhand side and normally have excellent short serve returns. When serving to a player who uses this style, avoid using serves with a lot of sidespin, especially if the opponent is using long pips. Try serving mid-depth serves to the backhand, mixing heavy backspin and no spin. Fast no-spin serves to the deep backhand often are very effective. Because players of this style often lack mobility, fast serves into the playing elbow can be very effective. Again, be

careful when serving sidespin if your opponent uses long pips. No-spin serves or short, heavy backspin serves work best.

The *all-around attacker* has the largest variety of strokes to choose from of any player in the game. Although having all of these options is a major strength, it can also be a weakness because this style of player can become confused about which stroke to use. When serving to an all-around attacker, the key is to be as unpredictable as possible. Continually mix the spin, speed, and placement of your serves to keep your opponent guessing.

Serving Strategy Drill. *Create Your Own Serving Plan*

On a piece of paper, list the basic playing styles discussed in this step. List your own personal serving strategy when playing against each style. Remember to list not only the type of serves to use but also their locations. Finally, write down your strategy when serving at the critical end part of the game.

Success Check

• Develop a serving plan for each style of play.

• Ask your playing partners or coach for feedback on your plan.
• Practice your plans when playing against the various styles, and adjust the plans when necessary.

Score Your Success

Develop a plan for each of the seven playing styles = 10 points

Your score ___

SUCCESS SUMMARY OF PERFORMING INTERMEDIATE SERVES

This step addressed how to make serves more deceptive, how to practice serves effectively, and how to use serves during match play. As you can see, the serve is a dominant force in table tennis. Improving your serve game is the quickest way to raising your overall level of play. Serve practice should be a component of every training session.

The drills in this step will help you practice the elements of serve deception and develop your own serving strategy. To see whether you are ready to move on to step 11, add up your drill scores. If you scored at least 30 points, you are ready to move on to step 11. If not, practice more to improve your scores.

Deceptive Serves Drills

1. One Heavy Backspin Serve, One Light Backspin Serve   ___ out of 10

2. Forehand Double-Motion Serves   ___ out of 10

3. High-Toss Serves   ___ out of 20

Serving Strategy Drill

1. Create Your Own Serving Plan   ___ out of 10

Total   **___ out of 50**

You now have all the technical skills you need to become a complete player. In step 11, you will learn the special skills and knowledge you need to become successfully involved in sanctioned tournament play.

Competing Successfully in Tournaments

By its definition, sport involves competition. Many sports include not only competition against an opponent but competition with yourself to achieve your best level of play. Many players perform well in their local clubs or leagues but have real problems achieving the same results under the pressure of tournament competition. Competing successfully in a tournament environment requires developing several special skills. This step provides the tools you need to get started on the road to becoming a successful tournament player.

CHOOSING A TOURNAMENT

Your first decision is where and when you will compete. USA Table Tennis (USATT) offers hundreds of sanctioned tournaments in cities across the United States every year. A sanctioned USATT tournament must meet certain standards, and all USATT rules and regulations are enforced. A complete list of these events, plus the standards, rules, and regulations, can be found at the USATT Web site (see The Sport of Table Tennis, page xix). Many other agencies, such as local recreation departments, colleges, and churches, offer nonsanctioned competitions. For the senior athlete, state and national Senior Olympic competitions are available.

Most tournaments offer a range of events for players at all levels. These events may be based on age, but most often they are open to players at various USATT rating levels. Players are al-lowed to play at their own rating levels and those above their levels. After you compete in your first sanctioned tournament, you are assigned a numerical rating that indicates your level against all other rated players. To play in a sanctioned tournament, you must become a member of the USATT. Your membership is good at all tournaments for one year, includes a subscription to *USATT Magazine*, and supports the growth of the sport in the United States.

Every player who has played in a sanctioned USATT tournament has an official rating. Ratings are adjusted after each tournament and are published both online and in *USATT Magazine*. Players are awarded points for winning matches and lose points for losing matches. The amount of points won or lost varies depending on the ratings of the two players involved (table 11.1).

For example, if player A, who is rated 1200, defeats player B, who is rated 1210, player A gains 8 points, increasing to 1208, and player B loses 8 points, decreasing to 1202.

After their first USATT tournament, players are given an initial rating based on their performance in that event. If you are playing in your first sanctioned tournament, check with the tournament director to see which events you are eligible to compete in. Additionally, players with exceptional gains following a tournament may have their ratings adjusted. This not only rewards them for their performances, but also reduces the rating losses sustained by their opponents. Player levels are determined based on USATT ratings (table 11.2).

Every sanctioned tournament publishes an official entry blank that contains all the information you need to know about the event including dates, starting times for the events, event descriptions, entry fees, prizes, types of equipment being used (tables and balls), venue descriptions and addresses, number of games for each match, event formats, names of tournament staff, referees' names, and much more. Take the time to read carefully all the information in the entry blank before you send in your entry.

Table 11.1   USATT Rating Chart

Point spread between players	Expected result (higher-rated player wins: number of points exchanged)	Upset result (lower-rated player wins: number of points exchanged)
0–12	8	8
13–37	7	10
38–62	6	13
63–87	5	16
88–112	4	20
113–137	3	25
138–162	2	30
163–187	2	35
188–212	1	40
213–237	1	45
238 and up	0	50

Used by permission of the USATT.

Table 11.2   Comparing Playing Levels With USATT Ratings

Rating	Level
Under 1000	Beginner
1100 to 1700	Intermediate
1800 to 2200	Advanced
2300 to 2500	Elite
2500 to 2700	National

UNDERSTANDING TOURNAMENT FORMATS

Although there are many possible event formats, three are the most common: round robin; knock-out, or single elimination; and round robin into knock-out.

In the round robin format (figure 11.1), players are placed in groups in which each player plays every other player in the group. The player with the best record in the group wins the event. If two players finish with the same record, the player who won the match between the two is the winner. In the case of a three-way tie, the tie is broken by figuring the ratio of games won and lost among the three tied players. If this still results in a tie, the next tiebreaker is a ratio of points won over points lost. As you can see,

keeping accurate scores is very important during round robin events.

In knock-out, or single elimination, events (figure 11.2), all players are placed into a single elimination draw. The top-seeded players are separated according to established rules. A player who loses is eliminated from the event.

A round robin into knock-out tournament combines the previous two formats. In figure 11.3, 16 players are divided into four round robin groups of equal strength. The winner of each group moves on to the knock-out stage. This format is very popular because it gives everyone the opportunity to play a minimum number of matches and still makes it possible to effectively handle a large number of entries.

Player names	Player numbers								Win/loss record	Ranking
	1	2	3	4	5	6	7	8		
1.	■									
2.		■								
3.			■							
4.				■						
5.					■					
6.						■				
7.							■			
8.								■		

Figure 11.1 Sample round robin tournament format.

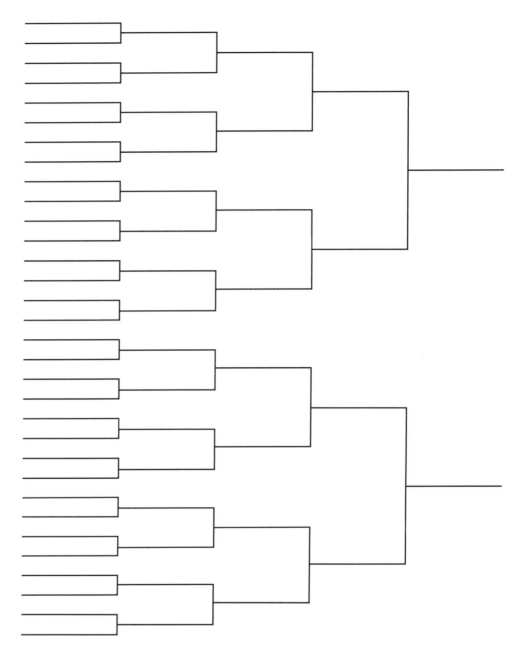

Figure 11.2 Sample knock-out, or single elimination, event.

GROUP 1
Round 1: 1 v. 16, 8 v. 9 Round 2: 1 v. 9, 8 v. 16 Round 3: 1 v. 8, 9 v. 16

Player names	Player numbers				Win/loss record	Ranking
	1	8	9	16		
1.						
8.						
9.						
16.						

GROUP 2
Round 1: 2 v. 15, 7 v. 10 Round 2: 2 v. 10, 7 v. 15 Round 3: 2 v. 7, 10 v. 15

Player names	Player numbers				Win/loss record	Ranking
	2	7	10	15		
2.						
7.						
10.						
15.						

GROUP 3
Round 1: 3 v. 14, 6 v. 11 Round 2: 3 v. 11, 6 v. 14 Round 3: 3 v. 6, 11 v. 14

Player names	Player numbers				Win/loss record	Ranking
	3	6	11	14		
3.						
6.						
11.						
14.						

GROUP 4
Round 1: 4 v. 13, 5 v. 12 Round 2: 4 v. 12, 5 v. 13 Round 3: 4 v. 5, 12 v. 13

Player names	Player numbers				Win/loss record	Ranking
	4	5	12	13		
4.						
5.						
12.						
13.						

Figure 11.3 Sample round robin into knock-out tournament.

GETTING THE MOST OUT OF YOUR TOURNAMENT EXPERIENCE

When evaluating your tournament performance, you need to consider much more than wins and losses. More important is what you learned that will help your future development. Here are some factors to consider when playing in a tournament to help ensure your success.

Setting Goals

To prepare for a tournament, you first need to understand what this particular tournament means to you. Tournaments are simply opportunities to evaluate where your game is at a particular time. With this concept in mind, the best goals are technical and psychological ones. They should be simple and reflect the actual techniques you have been working on. If you can focus on these goals, performance (and winning) will take care of itself. Here are some examples of match goals:

- I will be totally focused for every point of the match.
- I will relax by focusing on my breathing before every serve.
- I will have a plan for the placement of each serve.
- I will successfully land 90 percent of my first attacks on the table.

Creating Match Tools

I have my students prepare several written tools to take with them to tournaments. The first is a goal sheet. The second is a tactics sheet that describes their own styles of play, strengths and weaknesses, and tactics to use against the major styles of play. This is similar to the one you created in step 8 (page 146). Finally, they have a match evaluation form to fill out at the conclusion of each match (figure 11.4).

These tools will help you stay focused throughout the event and can also help you to learn from each match you play. The notes you keep will prove invaluable at the end of the tournament to help you and your coach prepare or update your next training plan.

Arriving Early and Preparing for Play

I always am amazed at the number of people who go to great trouble to attend a tournament and then show up only a few minutes before their first match. This is a sure way to have poor results. Every athlete needs adequate time in the venue to prepare before each match. If possible, try to arrive the night before the event and get in a practice session. Use this time to do the following:

- Get used to conditions such as change of altitude, tables, balls, flooring, and lighting
- Practice on a variety of tables and check conditions in various locations around the hall
- Try to meet the referee and tournament director and find the officials' desk
- Review the draws and schedule and make notes
- Arrange warm-up partners in advance, if possible

Always warm up properly using a routine that you have developed and practiced during training. Include both a physical warm-up and a table warm-up.

Playing, Scouting, and Resting

During competition, be aware of your hydration and nutrition needs. If possible, bring light snack foods and drinks with you. Many athletes forget to adequately drink and eat during competition. Try to plan your eating schedule based on your competition schedule, and keep track of the food and drink you consume.

Match Evaluation Form
for
(Your Name Here)

Tournament: _____ Date: _____

Event: _____ Round: _____

Opponent: _____ Rating: _____

Right- or left-handed: _____ Type of rubber: FH _____ BH _____

Opponent's style: Primary _____ Secondary _____

Game scores: _____

Technical Evaluations

Describe opponent's serve game (locations and patterns):

Describe opponent's receive game (strengths and weaknesses):

Describe opponent's most effective tactics (patterns):

Describe your most effective tactics (patterns):

Special notes:

Figure 11.4 Sample match evaluation form.

Try to get a look at your upcoming opponents. If this is not possible, try to find someone who has played them and ask some basic questions, such as the following:

- What is their basic style of play?
- What types of rubber—inverted, short pips, long pips, or antispin—are they using?
- What are their favorite serves and serve returns?
- What are their tendencies at critical times of the match?
- What are their strongest shots?

If you have enough time between matches, try to rest. Find a quiet corner, or go outside the hall for a while. Remember, you should never leave the venue without first getting the permission of the referee.

Bring several changes of clothes if you are going to be in the playing hall for a long time. Putting on fresh clothes will help you feel physically and psychologically refreshed. Don't forget to bring some small towels to use during matches to keep your hands dry.

After each match, fill out your match evaluation form or make some notes. You will find this information invaluable at the end of the event.

FOLLOWING MATCH ETIQUETTE

Always check in at the control desk at least five minutes before the scheduled starting time of your match.

Before they warm up, players are allowed to examine each other's rackets to see what types of rubber are being used.

Warm-up time is limited to two minutes, and then the match should start. Use this brief time to get used to the playing characteristics of your court. You should be warmed up and ready to play before you report to your match.

Do not walk into the adjoining courts during play. If your ball goes into another court, wait until the point is over and ask for the ball to be returned.

If a ball enters your court from another table during play, either player can call a let, and the point is played over. A player cannot call for a let after finishing the point.

The server should call the score before the start of each point, giving the server's score

first. This is very important to avoid arguments over the score.

Players are allowed a one-minute break between games. They are required to stay within the court area.

Players can receive coaching only between games or during time-outs. Each player is entitled to one time-out per match, and it can be called by either the player or the coach. The time-out is limited to one minute, or less if the player who called the time-out is ready to resume.

The majority of matches will not have an umpire. In the case of an argument over rules or score, request that an umpire be assigned for the rest of your match. Do not argue with your opponent or ask the opinions of spectators.

At the end of the match, always shake your opponent's hand. If an umpire is present, shake the umpire's hand as well.

If no umpire is present, the winner of the match should fill out the score card and return it to the control desk.

PLAYING THE MENTAL GAME

As your skill progresses, you will find the mental part of the game becoming more important. In addition to technical and physical training, successful athletes must learn to master their emotions and thoughts. Many talented players have

found this to be their major hurdle in achieving elite status. Learning the simple mental skills addressed in this section will help you perform your best during competition.

Learning to Relax

Table tennis is a quick sport that requires you to be in a relaxed state to play well. A simple relaxation method is to concentrate on your breathing. Develop the habit of taking several deep breaths from your diaphragm before starting each point. Breathe in through your nose and out through your mouth. As you breathe out, visualize all the tension leaving your body.

Developing Personal Routines

Good match players develop a number of routines during practice that they can carry with them to tournaments. Following are some examples:

- Going to bed at a set hour the night before a tournament.

- Arriving at the playing hall at a set time before matches start.

- Eating a standard prematch meal.

- Always warming up the same way before each match.

- Using personal serve and receive rituals. Good players always go through a series of movements before serving or receiving serve. These rituals help them focus their minds before the start of each point. Having these familiar routines will help you feel more comfortable in unfamiliar settings.

Focusing on Your Strategy, Not on Winning

Everyone wants to win, but focusing on winning often leads to nervous play and poor results. Try to concentrate on the basic strategy you are trying to implement, and play each point one at a time. Make sure you have a plan in mind before starting each point. Focus on that plan, and let the winning take care of itself.

Focusing on What You Can Control

During the match, you have no control over the behavior of your opponent, crowd noise, lucky nets or edges, the umpire, or playing conditions. Focusing on such things can be counterproductive to achieving good results. Always focus on your own emotions and play, because these are the only elements under your control.

Controlling Your Psychological Energy Level

Every player has an optimum level of mental energy needed for playing at the highest level. When you are in the mental zone, you feel focused, relaxed, and energized. Sometimes, though, you will feel as though you have too little or too much energy.

Signs that your mental energy level is too low include boredom, lethargy, and disinterest. When this occurs, try to increase your energy level by increasing your movement around the table, reminding yourself of your goals, and increasing your heart rate.

Signs that your mental energy level is too high are muscle tension, poor concentration, and shallow breathing. When this occurs, try to calm yourself by concentrating on your breathing and relaxing your muscles.

SUCCESS SUMMARY OF PERFORMING SUCCESSFULLY IN TOURNAMENTS

This step provided the information you need to begin competition in organized tournament play. Tournament play can be a rewarding experience, especially if you take the time to prepare yourself properly. Tournaments offer the opportunity not only to learn from each match you play, but also to watch higher-level players and learn from them as well. Finally, you will have the opportunity to make new and often lifelong friends at these events.

This step marks the end of this book but the start of your journey into the sport of table tennis. If you follow the steps to success in this book, your journey will be a rich and fulfilling one.

◲ Glossary

all-around attacker—A player who can adjust his game to take advantage of an opponent's weaknesses.

antispin—An inverted rubber sheet with a slick surface that produces mostly low-spin returns. It usually has a dead sponge underneath and is used mostly for defensive shots. Also known as *anti*.

attacking chopper—A player who uses a style of play based on mixing defensive chopping strokes with strong forehand topspin strokes.

backhand—A stroke executed with the racket to the left of the left elbow for a right-handed player, the reverse for a left-handed player.

backspin—A type of spin used mostly on defensive shots. To produce backspin, the racket contacts the ball below its center with a downward, chopping action. While the ball is traveling forward, it rotates back toward the player who hit it. This is also called *underspin*.

blade—The wood part of the racket without covering.

block—A quick, off-the-bounce return of an aggressive drive executed by holding the racket in the ball's path.

chop—A defensive return of a drive or topspin with backspin, usually done well away from the table (see *backspin*).

chop block—A block in which the racket moves downward at contact to create backspin.

close-to-the-table defender—A player who uses a style of play based on defensive blocking to force errors from the opponent.

counterdrive—A drive made against a drive.

counterdriver—A player who uses a style of play based on consistent counterdriving from both backhand and forehand.

countersmash—To smash a smash (see *smash*).

countertopspin (counterloop)—To loop a loop (see *loop*).

crosscourt—From corner to corner diagonally.

default—Being disqualified from a match for any reason.

double-motion serve—A deceptive serve in which the server makes two quick motions at the ball in an attempt to disguise where contact is made on the ball.

down the line—Along one side of the table, parallel to the side lines.

drive stroke—A fast, attacking stroke that carries minimum topspin.

drop shot—A ball that drops short over the net so that the opponent has trouble reaching it; often used to return a short serve or when an opponent is back from the table.

expedite rule—A rule that comes into play when a game is unfinished at the end of 10 minutes, unless both players have reached 9 points. A point is awarded to the receiver who returns 13 consecutive shots after expedite has been called. Players alternate serves after expedite has been called.

five-ball training system—A system of training focused on the first five strokes that can occur in every point.

flip—An aggressive topspin return that lands near the net; a short ball.

footwork—How a person moves to make a shot.

force contact—Contact that results when the racket moves forward when contacting the ball. This type of contact produces forward speed on the ball.

forehand—Any stroke executed with the racket to the right of the elbow for a right-handed player, to the left for a left-handed player.

free hand—The hand not holding the racket.

friction contact—Contact that results when the racket brushes the ball at contact, imparting spin to the ball.

game—The first person to reach 11 points with at least a 2-point margin wins the game.

hard rubber—A type of racket covering with pips-out rubber but no sponge underneath. It was the most common covering for many years until the development of sponge rubber, but is now rarely used.

high-toss serve—A serve in which the ball is thrown high into the air. This increases both spin and deception.

International Table Tennis Federation (ITTF)—The international governing body for the sport of table tennis.

inverted sponge—The most common racket covering. It consists of a sheet of pimpled rubber on top of a layer of sponge. The pips point inward, toward the sponge, so the surface is smooth. This is the opposite of pips-out sponge, in which the pips point outward, away from the sponge.

kill shot—A stroke executed with maximum speed. See *smash*.

knock-out—A competition system of play in which players are eliminated when they lose a single match; also called single elimination.

let—A suspension of play for the purpose of replaying the point. A player can call a let when play is interrupted for any reason during a rally.

let serve—A let that is called when a serve nicks the net. As with other lets, the serve is taken over again. The let serve is the most common type of let.

lob—A high, defensive return of a smash, usually done with topspin or sidespin.

long-pips rubber—A type of pips-out rubber on which the pips are long and thin and bend on contact with the ball. Long-pips rubber returns the ball with whatever spin was on it at contact, which is very difficult to play against if you aren't used to it.

loop—A heavy topspin shot usually considered the most important shot in the game. Many players specialize in either looping or returning the loop.

match—A contest that consists of any odd number of games. Most often a table tennis match consists of either the best three of five games or the best four of seven games.

mid-distance aggressive looper—A player who prefers to play from a few feet (around 1 m) back from the table with strong forehand and backhand topspin strokes.

multiball training—A system of practice drills in which a feeder feeds many balls continuously to a person doing a set drill. There is no replay of the ball.

no-spin return—A return with little or no spin.

pen-hold grip—A type of grip used mostly by Asian players. It gives the best possible forehand but the most awkward backhand of the conventional grips.

pips-out pen-hold style—A classic Chinese style of play, featuring strong pen-hold forehand drives and quick backhand blocks.

playing surface—The top of the table, including the edges.

power looper—A player who uses a very aggressive style of play based on powerful forehand topspin attacking strokes.

punch block—A block in which the racket pushes through the ball at contact to add speed.

push—A backspin return of a backspin stroke. The stroke is usually defensive and executed close to or over the table.

racket—The implement used to hit the ball; the blade plus the covering.

racket hand—The hand that holds the racket.

rally—The hitting of the ball back and forth, commencing with the serve and ending when a point is won.

rating—The numerical representation of a player's level of play.

receive—The return of a serve.

referee—The tournament official in charge; the one responsible for ensuring that the event is run according to the rules and for settling any rule disputes.

robot—A ball-throwing machine that allows a player to practice without a partner.

round robin—A competition format in which players are put in small groups in which all players play each other.

rubber—The racket covering; sometimes refers only to the rubber on top of a sponge base.

rubber cleaner—A product used to keep the surface of inverted rubber clean.

sandwich rubber—A sponge base covered by a sheet of rubber with pips that point either in or out. If the pips point in, it is an inverted sponge. If the pips point out, it is a pips-out sponge.

serve—The first stroke in each point. The server tosses the ball from the palm of the hand and strikes it with the racket as it comes down.

shake-hands grip—The most popular grip. It gives the best balance of forehand and backhand strokes.

short-pips rubber—A type of racket covering that consists of a sheet of pips-out rubber on top of a layer of sponge. The pips point outward, the opposite of inverted. Also called pips-out rubber.

sidespin—A type of spin in which the ball spins from left to right or right to left as it moves forward. This is used most often in conjunction with either topspin or backspin.

sidespin block—A block with sidespin added at contact.

smash—A ball that is hit with enough speed to prevent the opponent from making a return; also called a kill shot or a put-away shot.

speed glue—A type of glue that can be put under a sheet of table tennis sponge to make it faster and create more spin. This is now illegal under ITTF and USATT rules.

spin—The rotation of the ball.

sponge—The bouncy rubber material used in sandwich covering under a sheet of rubber with pips. It revolutionized the game and ended the hard rubber age of the 1950s.

stroke—Any shot used in the game, including the serve.

timing—The ability to choose the point of contact with the ball that will produce the desired stroke.

topspin—The type of spin produced when the racket brushes the ball while it is moving upward. A ball with topspin spins away from the player after contact.

topspin block—A block with added topspin.

topspin stroke (loop)—An attacking stroke in which the racket contacts the ball while moving from low to high to produce topspin. Heavy topspin strokes are often referred to as loops.

umpire—The official who keeps score and enforces rules during a match.

underspin—See *backspin*.

USA Table Tennis (USATT)—The governing body of the sport of table tennis in the United States.

◧ About the Author

Richard McAfee has a lifelong commitment to table tennis. In his early years, McAfee was a successful player, winning many singles and doubles events including the 1972 U.S. Open Class B Championship and the Southern Open Men's Singles title. Later McAfee began to focus on his true passion of coaching. He has coached national champions in each of the past three decades, seven world-ranked players, and two Olympians.

In 1994 McAfee was named competition manager for Table Tennis at the 1996 Atlanta Olympic Games. This led to further management positions on the international scene and earned him the International Olympic Committee's Olympic Merit Award. He is also certified by USA Table Tennis (USATT) as a national-level coach, their highest level. Honors include the 2004 U.S. Olympic Committee Doc Counsilman Science Award for table tennis, the 2003 Georgia AAU Coach of the Year award for table tennis, and the 1999 U.S. Committee Developmental Coach of the Year Award for table tennis. McAfee was inducted in to the U.S. Table Tennis Hall of Fame in 2005. In 2009, he was appointed chairperson of the USATT's National Coaching Advisory Committee. He continues to travel around the world conducting coaching education courses for the International Table Tennis Federation.

STEPS TO SUCCESS SPORTS SERIES

The *Steps to Success Sports Series* is the most extensively researched and carefully developed set of books ever published for teaching and learning sports skills.

Each of the books offers a complete progression of skills, concepts, and strategies that are carefully sequenced to optimize learning for students, teaching for sport-specific instructors, and instructional program design techniques for future teachers.

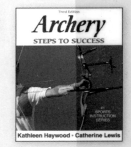

The *Steps to Success Sports Series* includes:

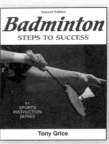
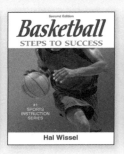
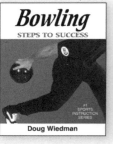

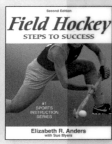

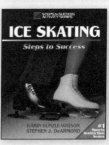
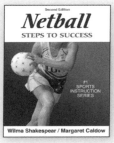
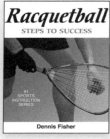
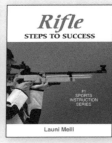

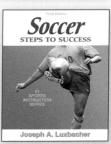

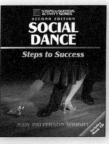

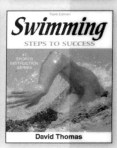

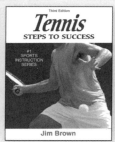
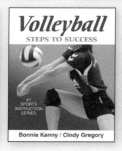
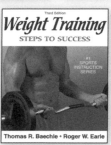

To place your order, U.S. customers call
TOLL FREE **1-800-747-4457**
In Canada call 1-800-465-7301
In Australia call 08 8372 0999
In Europe call +44 (0) 113 255 5665
In New Zealand call 0064 9 448 1207
or visit **www.HumanKinetics.com/StepstoSuccess**

HUMAN KINETICS
The Premier Publisher for Sports & Fitness
P.O. Box 5076, Champaign, IL 61825-5076